T0384107

Leadership for Intellectual Disability Service

Motivating Change and Improvement

Leadership for Intellectual Disability Service

Motivating Change and Improvement

By

Fintan Sheerin and Elizabeth A. Curtis

Routledge
Taylor & Francis Group

A PRODUCTIVITY PRESS BOOK

First edition published in 2019
by Routledge/Productivity Press
52 Vanderbilt Avenue, 11th Floor New York, NY 10017
2 Park Square, Milton Park, Abingdon, Oxon OX14 4RN, UK

© 2019 by Taylor & Francis Group, LLC
Routledge/Productivity Press is an imprint of Taylor & Francis Group, an Informa business

No claim to original U.S. Government works

Printed on acid-free paper

International Standard Book Number-13: 978-0-8153-9084-8 (Hardback)
International Standard Book Number-13: 978-1-351-17240-0 (eBook)

Library of Congress Cataloging-in-Publication Data

Names: Sheerin, Fintan, author. | Curtis, Elizabeth A., author.
Title: Leadership for intellectual disability service : motivating change and improvement / Fintan Sheerin and Elizabeth A. Curtis.
Description: 1 Edition. | New York : Routledge, [2019] | Includes bibliographical references. |
Identifiers: LCCN 2018058389 (print) | LCCN 2019015444 (ebook) | ISBN 9781351172400 (e-Book) | ISBN 9780815390848 (hardback : alk. paper)
Subjects: LCSH: People with mental disabilities--Services for. | Intellectual disability facilities. | Leadership.
Classification: LCC HV3001.A4 (ebook) | LCC HV3001.A4 S53 2019 (print) | DDC 362.3068/4--dc23
LC record available at https://lccn.loc.gov/2018058389

**Visit the Taylor & Francis Web site at
http://www.taylorandfrancis.com**

Contents

Preface

There are several books with the word leadership in their titles and we are in no doubt that there will be several more by the time the current book is published. While there may be several reasons for this, our view is that leadership is relevant and important because it affects all of us at some stage in our working and personal lives. Furthermore, leadership is an evolving concept which means that traditional ways of doing things may need to change to accommodate new knowledge. Writing about leadership Hughes and colleagues (Hughes et al., 2006: V) remind us that 'often the only difference between chaos and a smoothly functioning operation is leadership'. This emphasis on the relevance and significance of leadership is sanctioned by other authors including the King's Fund (2015). As editors of this book, we also endorse the view that leadership is central to nursing and healthcare and are in no doubt about its significance in creating a healthy work climate and ensuring that the care provided to clients and patients is safe, compassionate and of a high standard. In addition to its advantages and importance, leadership gains further kudos during times of change. Organisations must constantly innovate and embrace new ideas and ways of doing things if they wish to remain competitive and survive. Change, however, can be challenging and many initiatives fail because of inadequate preparation, low motivation and resistance. This book offers readers useful insights for leading and managing change.

Why this Book?

Leadership in Intellectual Disability: Motivating Change and Improvement argues for alternative and innovative approaches to leadership in intellectual disability service provision. It does this in the light of service scandals including Winterborne View (UK), Oswald D. Heck (USA), Áras Attracta (Ireland) and many others. The book explores the failed leadership issues underpinning such debacles and then examines how the context for intellectual disability service provision has changed. It then proposes alternative models for service leadership that are contiguous with the changed landscape, ending with exemplary vignettes outlining situations where such innovative change is happening.

Recent reviews of intellectual disability service provision in Ireland and the work of the 'Strengthening the Commitment' group in the United Kingdom have both highlighted the need for leadership education and training in health and social service provision. Such education is sorely lacking and this book, therefore, seeks to address this gap.

The aims of the book are to:

- Operationalise leadership for change within the provision of intellectual disability services, across health, social care and education.
- Reflect on the theory and practice of leadership, in the current service contexts, in order to stimulate change among practitioners, researchers, activists and academics.
- Increase knowledge about leadership and change within intellectual disability, an area that has been sparsely explored.
- Address leadership in the context of significant service failures across a number of countries and will explore practical and innovative ways in which such leadership shortcomings can be addressed.

This book has some stand out features that include:

- This book, which is about operationalising leadership for change within the discipline of intellectual disability, is designed for practitioners and academics and will be specifically important for managers, professionals involved in providing client/patient care or those who plan to take on leadership roles.
- It reflects the theory and practice of leadership in order to satisfy the needs of both practitioners and academics.
- Leadership has a vast literature generally, as well as in healthcare, but despite this huge interest and prolific amount of material on the subject, few books have addressed the issue of leadership and change within intellectual disability.
- It uniquely considers leadership in the context of significant service failures across a number of countries and explores practical and innovative ways in which such leadership shortcomings can be addressed.

The book is written primarily for health and social care practitioners from the discipline of intellectual disability but should be useful to carers and health professionals from other disciplines given that some of the issues addressed are relevant to all health personnel. Moreover, all leaders, irrespective of title or position, should find some useful tips on leadership, innovation and change.

Structure

Section I Background and Context sets out the backdrop for the book, identifying the development of leadership approaches within intellectual disability services, by reflecting on historical and attitudinal contexts. This is undertaken in the light of poor standards and questionable leadership. It then considers how constant changes in health and social services, societal perspectives and human rights have resulted in a requirement for new models of leadership to be employed.

Section II Leadership for Improving and Energising considers what is known about leadership, drawing on various theories and exploring the role of motivation in achieving leadership change. It examines the psychological basis for leadership and seeks to explore how 'ownership' and power dynamics can affect the successful implementation of change.

Section III Innovating Through Change presents two innovative approaches which demonstrate how leadership change was achieved in a number of areas of intellectual disability provision. It draws on the experiences of a leadership expert and of leaders who have successfully developed initiatives in social and education arenas.

Section IV Application seeks to provide insight into some of the issues that present when participative and distributive leadership are being enacted. It seeks to draw together some of the theory and recommended approaches from the earlier part of the book, by allowing leaders to tell us, in their own words, about experiences which resulted in positive leadership outcomes. Four exemplars of excellence are presented and demonstrate the importance of the following concepts: (1) motivation; (2) collaboration; (3) inclusion; and (4) innovation. These are presented in the style preferred by the specific leaders and so are based on description, report and interview.

Overall, we feel that this book provides an important starting point for the consideration of leadership in intellectual disability service provision and we hope that it will foster further work in its regard.

Fintan Sheerin and Elizabeth A. Curtis

Reference

Hughes, R.L., Ginnett, R.C. and Curphy, G.J. (2006) *Leadership: Enhancing the Lessons of Experience.* (5th ed.) Boston: McGraw Hill.

Acknowledgements

The authors wish to gratefully acknowledge all who contributed to this book, particularly those who submitted their exemplars for Section IV: Lorraine Ledger, Anne-Marie O'Reilly, Anna Logan, Maximo Pimentel and Brendan Broderick. We would also like to thank Dr. Phil Halligan, of University College Dublin, who provided an independent perspective.

Contributors

Prof. Martin Beirne
Adam Smith Business School, University of Glasgow,
Glasgow, G12 8QQ, United Kingdom.

Martin is Professor of Management and Organisational
Behaviour at the University of Glasgow. His research and
publications focus on participative forms of management and
work organization, with particular current attention to leadership reform and distributed change agency in health care and
the arts. His recent publications include articles on employee
resilience and activism to address inequalities and secure
improvements in the experience and effectiveness of work.
Martin.Beirne@glasgow.ac.uk

Dr. Elizabeth A. Curtis
School of Nursing and Midwifery, University of Dublin,
Trinity College Dublin, Dublin 2. Ireland.

Elizabeth is a member of the academic team in the School
of Nursing and Midwifery, Trinity College Dublin. She qualified as a general nurse in London and worked in the discipline of neurosciences in the National Health Service (NHS).
Her research interests are varied and include job satisfaction
and leadership. Published books include *Research Success
in Nursing and Health Care: A Guide to Doing Your Higher
Degree* (2008), *Delegation: A Short Primer for the Practicing
Nurse* (2009), *Quantitative Health Research: Issues and Methods*

(2013) and *Leadership and Change for the Health Professional* (2017). Five years ago, Elizabeth set up a Leadership Network Group to promote and expand work on leadership in nursing.

curtise@tcd.ie

Dr. Morgan Danaher
Department of Education and Health Sciences,
University of Limerick, Ireland.

Morgan is Director of Services with a global Human Capital Management organization responsible for the design, delivery and control of complex software and service solutions in this field. In addition, Morgan works as a lecturer in leadership and entrepreneurship at the University of Limerick while also acting as supervisor to a number of Master's students, at the university. He has a number of publications in the areas of entrepreneurship and education and his primary research interests centre around the role of self-regulation in mastery over a wide variety of contexts.

morgan.danaher@ul.ie

Dr. Colin Griffiths
School of Nursing and Midwifery, University of Dublin,
Trinity College Dublin, Dublin 2. Ireland.

Colin graduated from training as a registered nurse for people with intellectual disability in 1977. He then worked for 23 years in different centres in Ireland. In 2002 he joined Trinity College as a lecturer in intellectual disability nursing. His PhD was undertaken in Trinity College and looked at how people with profound and complex intellectual disability communicate. He currently teaches inclusion and communication and focusses specifically on how nurses can promote best practice in the context of distributed leadership in services.

cgriffi@tcd.ie

Debra Hart, MS
Institute for Community Inclusion, University of
Massachusetts, Boston. United States of America.

Debra is Director of the Education and Transition team for
the Institute for Community Inclusion at the University of
Massachusetts, Boston. She has over 30 years of experience,
working as a Principal Investigator on over 40 different state
and national projects. Debra's work has been with students
with disabilities, their families and professionals to support
youth in becoming valued members of their community via
participation in inclusive K-12 education, inclusive higher education and competitive integrated employment. More recently,
she has focused on transition-aged youth related work with
State Educational Agencies, Local Educational Agencies and
adult service agencies both in Massachusetts and nationwide.
Debra has also written a number of publications in the area
of higher education for students with intellectual disability
including co-authoring a book, *Think College! Postsecondary
Education Options for Students with Intellectual Disabilities*,
book chapters and numerous peer reviewed journal articles.
Debra.Hart@umb.edu

Dr. Christine Linehan
UCD Centre for Disability Studies, School of Psychology,
University College Dublin, Belfield, Dublin 4. Ireland.

Christine is Associate Professor with the School of Psychology,
University College Dublin and Director of the UCD Centre
for Disability Studies. Christine is also an Honorary Senior
Lecturer with the Tizard Centre, University of Kent, UK.
Before moving to UCD, Christine was Director of the National
Institute for Intellectual Disability at Trinity College Dublin and
a Visiting Senior Research Fellow at Trinity's School of Social
Work and Social Policy. Prior to this, Christine was employed
as Senior Research Officer with the National Disability

Authority, the statutory body providing advice on disability practice and policy to the Irish Government.

christine.linehan@ucd.ie

Prof. Ruth Northway
Faculty of Life Sciences and Education, University of South Wales, Pontypridd, CF37 1DL. United Kingdom.

Ruth is Professor of Learning Disability Nursing and Head of Research in the Faculty of Life Sciences and Education, University of South Wales. An intellectual disabilities nurse by professional background she supported people with intellectual disabilities in a range of residential and community settings prior to moving to work in nurse education. In her current role she teaches across undergraduate and postgraduate courses. Her research interests include the health and well-being of people with intellectual disabilities and safeguarding those who may be vulnerable to abuse. She is Editor in Chief of the *Journal of Intellectual Disabilities*.

ruth.northway@southwales.ac.uk

Dr. Maria Paiewonsky
Institute for Community Inclusion, University of Massachusetts, Boston. United States of America.

Maria is a programme manager and transition specialist at the Institute for Community Inclusion. She also serves as Director of the Massachusetts Transition Leadership Initiative, a personnel preparation programme that prepared master's Level Transition Specialists at the University of Massachusetts Boston. Maria has coordinated numerous secondary and transition related projects and works with teachers, interdisciplinary team members, students and families to develop positive and inclusive college, work and community outcomes. She has also facilitated a number of inclusive research projects with students with disabilities to assist them in evaluating their own transition and college experiences. Most recently, she has

coordinated a federally funded project called 'Think College Transition', partnering with three institutes of higher education and numerous partnering school districts to implement, research and evaluate an inclusive dual enrolment transition model of services for students with intellectual disability.
Maria.Paiewonsky@umb.edu

Dr. Patrick Ryan
Department of Psychology, University of Limerick, Ireland.

Patrick has worked as a clinical psychologist for 22 years in general mental health services and in intellectual disability services, with a specialist interest in trauma and offending behaviour. He has worked at the University of Limerick since 2005, first as Director of the Doctoral Programme in Clinical Psychology and subsequently as Head of Education & Professional Studies, and then Head of Psychology. He has supervised 50 practice and research PhD theses to completion, authored books, book chapters and journal papers. Since 2001, he is chairperson of a supported employment company for people who experience disability.
patrick.ryan@ul.ie

Dr. Fintan Sheerin
School of Nursing and Midwifery, University of Dublin, Trinity College Dublin, Dublin 2. Ireland.

Fintan is Associate Professor in and Head of Intellectual Disability Nursing at the School of Nursing and Midwifery in Trinity College Dublin. His research has largely focused on engagement, accessibility and well-being, seeking to address the issues which impact on both. He leads the mental health component of IDS-TILDA and is guiding the analysis of data gathered to date and exploring the future focus of data in that regard. Fintan is a social activist in respect of various groups of people who find themselves on the margins of society.

He was the consultant to the Irish RTÉ television documentary, *Inside Bungalow* 3, which exposed abuse of people with an intellectual disability at *Áras Attracta* leading to successful prosecutions. He has published widely, spoken at many international conferences and has contributed to a number of books. He is a Fellow of the European Academy of Nursing Science.

sheerinf@tcd.ie

BACKGROUND AND CONTEXT

Chapter 1

Leadership and Intellectual Disability Services

Fintan Sheerin

Contents

Chapter Topics

- **Brief historical backdrop to service provision in Ireland, UK and the United States and the factors that contextualised these**
- **Power and management of institutional services/ hospitals/asylums**
- **Increasing impact from outside: movement from largely biomedical approaches to more social ones in the 1950s with voices of families and service users starting to impact on management**
- **Emergent leadership in new differentiating models of health, education and social support**
- **Exemplars of service, and by association, leadership breakdown**
- **Leading out of the margin: challenges to participatory leadership.**

Introduction

Recent narrative on service provision to people who experience intellectual disability* has been increasingly (and correctly) framed within a context of human rights. The main impetus for this was the signing of the United Nations Convention on the Rights of Persons with Disabilities (UNCRPD) in 2006 and its subsequent ratification by many countries. The production of such a declaration spoke to the realisation that the rights of people who experience intellectual disability are often arbitrarily denied. Furthermore, it located such deprivations of rights in outdated perspectives on human diversity, and management of the people themselves, in approaches which focused on deviance and abnormality.

---

* The term 'people who experience intellectual disability' is employed purposefully as it is consistent with a rights-based perspective on intellectual disability.

Whereas it is clear that the UNCRPD has led to an increased awareness and enactment of the human rights of many people who experience disability, people with intellectual impairment, as evidenced by scandals across a number of countries, often continue to experience significant denial and abuse of their human rights.

This chapter will consider the historical bases for perspectives which resulted in – and indeed maintain – the repression of human rights for these people. It will explore attempts to break free from restrictive approaches to service and uncover the models of leadership that have driven past and current responses to the needs of people who experience intellectual disability. Finally, it will look to the adoption of participatory models of leadership which may offer the hope of service responses grounded in greater inclusion.

Building a Service Model of Oppression: The Historical Basis

Prejudice exists at all levels of society, finding its basis in over-generalised, learned attitudes towards individuals, who are perceived not to conform with what is adjudged to be normal by those who hold power in that society (Young, 1990). These attitudes may be directed at any 'deviant' group or individual on the grounds of race, religion, sex, gender identity and orientation, impairment, disfigurement, behaviour, ethnicity, weight, area of residence, employment status and class, among others (ibid.). Such stereotyping of individuals may further manifest itself in them being treated unequally, solely on account of their membership of that 'deviant' group. Such has been the situation of people with intellectual impairment throughout the ages (Metzler, 2016). Historical accounts of how societies responded to the realities of intellectual and mental impairment often focus on a number of time periods: the Greco-Roman world; the pre-industrial agrarian societies;

industrialism; and the scientific revolution (Priestley, 1999). Many such descriptions of ancient times relate stories of infanticide and, whilst these are likely true, they are probably only partially true, referring to those born with visible difference, as many would not have displayed 'difference' in ability, behaviour and development until childhood (Metzler, 2016). What is clear is that such differences were often to some degree tolerated, although as sources of amusement for others in society (Sheerin, 1998). Judaeo-Christian scriptures, which significantly influenced perspectives in many parts of the world, similarly contextualised difference and impairment negatively, explaining them as punishments wrought by God in response to individuals' or societies' sinfulness (Sheerin, 2013a), and thus, contributed to the development of stigma.

Pre-industrial societies were built largely around peasant agriculture, although there were some centres of trade and manufacture. Education was principally the realm of the aristocracy, with most of the peasantry unable to read or write (Giddens, 2009). In such an agrarian context, the emphasis was on work rather than on education, and the reality of intellectual impairment was not a visible one. Those with multiple and complex impairments probably did not survive pregnancy, and if they did, they likely succumbed to the high rates of infant mortality (Worsley, 1992). Those who did survive had, in present terms, mild to moderate degrees of impairment, with little physical incapacitation.

The industrial revolution and consequent growth of cities increased the demand for educated and trained individuals (Mitch, 2018). Developing educational responses highlighted cohorts of people whose learning needs could not be met by such models. This was one factor that highlighted the existence of people with intellectual impairment, a cohort who formed a significant portion of the underclass, gravitating towards the poor law institutions (Wright, 2000). This further singled them out as a group that would place increasing demands on societal resources.

Concurrent developments in scientific knowledge compounded the problems of those with intellectual and other impairments. Advances in the understanding of genetics and evolution impacted societal thought challenging the long-held social beliefs that had been handed down by philosophers and theologians (Worsley, 1992). Christians had, for example, held to the literal interpretation of mankind's creation, as recounted in the book of Genesis. Darwin's suggestion that humans had evolved from animals, questioned the divine nature of humanity, leading to concerted religious opposition (Worsley, 1992). While most people had hitherto noted that 'like begets like, but imperfectly' (Gribben, 1993: 27), it was not until the late 1800s that the mechanics of genetics became widely known. However, this limited understanding of genetics and evolution melded with the prevalent perspectives on those with intellectual impairment to produce an argument that, if the survival of the fittest is the norm, the unfit (including people with intellectual impairment) should not be allowed to procreate, as this would lead to a preponderance of such persons in society, threatening social security (Tredgold, 1929 cited in Brandon, 1957: 711). This was based on the erroneous presumption that the children of parents with intellectual impairment would always themselves have intellectual impairment (Sheerin et al., 2013). These ideas were also based on a deeply held belief that 'all poor, feebleminded women at large become mothers of illegitimate (feebleminded) children soon after reaching the age of puberty' (Neff et al., 1915 cited in Brandon, 1957: 711); a throwback to the Christian perspective on the fallen woman (the *Magdalene*).

It was within the above context that formal societal responses to those with intellectual impairment developed. These typically took the form of large institutions within which all needs were addressed: health, social and educational. The model of leadership was, accordingly, matched to the service model.

Institutionalisation and Oppression

In order to stem multiplication of the 'unfit' and its perceived threat to society, prophylactic institutionalisation was commenced, driven by eugenic ideals, segregating those with intellectual impairment from society, and in many situations, through sterilisation, removing the possibility of them having a reproductive future (Reilly, 2015). Rafter (1992) argued that the eugenics movement in the United States, under the leadership of Josephine Lowell, served the purpose of criminalising the fact of being female and 'feebleminded'. This is confirmed by the stated view of the Newark Custodial Asylum that the uncontrolled female body was 'immoral, diseased, irrational, mindless' (Rafter, 1992: 25). The history of institutionalisation in Ireland mirrors that in other western countries with two main exceptions: the care was taken on not by the state but by Roman Catholic religious congregations, and there was no formal policy of sterilisation. It is curious however, that, while not formally influenced by the eugenics movement, these institutions bore a stark similarity to those of the eugenicists, both in their segregating policies, as well as in the austerity of their regimens. Indeed, Sheerin et al. (2013) have described this as religious eugenics for, in order to prevent 'the incitement to licentious thoughts and feelings which the presence of females serves to arouse' (Eyre, 1948 quoted in Robins, 1986: 135), the institutions enacted sexual segregation and took on the characteristics of total institutions (Goffman, 1961). Irrespective of their location, such institutions served to encompass the total daily experience of their inmates, depriving them of their individuality and exposing them to coercion and rebuttal. On a broader scale, institutional segregation denied people with intellectual impairments their civil rights, their potential for development and their opportunity to partake in everyday life; thus, removing them, on every level, to the margins of society.

It is arguable that the pervasive model of service delivery in the 20th century was one which was based on segregation, marginalisation and control. Despite being often presented from a medical perspective, it *managed problems* rather than seeking any real solutions for the 'patients'. And, while this looked quite sensible and caring from the healthcare perspective, Sheerin (2013b) has proposed that, when it is examined from other points of view, it smacked of oppression. Thus, he coined the term *Oppression Model* of service delivery, proffering a view that brings into focus the role of intellectual disability service, and the workforce therein, in subjugating the development of people with intellectual impairment. Within this model, people with intellectual impairment are oppressed individuals who, for centuries, have been cast into historical deviancy roles, and marginalised through processes of segregation and congregation (Sheerin, 1998, 2013b; Sheerin and Sines, 1999). This, allied to fundamentalist attitudes, led to them becoming objects of dread and of fear, 'immoral, diseased, irrational, mindless' (Rafter, 1992: 25). Such views and responses to persons with intellectual disabilities served to foster dehumanisation, leading to the point whereby the central focus of service provision became one of control and the means of control – means not always acceptable in mainstream society – became sanitised within the context of the professionalised practice (Ntinas, 2007). These things happened because, as Judith Klein, director of the Open Society Mental Health Initiative, said of atrocities committed against children with intellectual disabilities in Bulgarian state homes, 'these people don't count as people' (Klein quoted by Brunwasser, 2010).

It was within this context that people with intellectual impairment have repeatedly come to accept that their reality is different from that of other human beings. They became objects of charity (UN, 2010) 'extending their hands' (Freire, 1996: 27) to receive the generosity of others. It is arguable that this marginalisation not only physically separated them from society; it also allowed for their movement out of societal consciousness so that they essentially became 'forgotten' by society. Thus, the virtues embodied in civic republicanism, 'virtues of participation, democracy, liberty, equality and social solidarity' (Taskforce on Active Citizenship, 2007: 3), did not apply, and *charity*, rather than *solidarity* was afforded those in institutions (Sheerin, 2013b). Freire (1996) proposed that this form of charity was in fact false generosity in its essence and antonymic to solidarity. He argued that such false generosity, deriving from the oppressors, actually benefitted the conscience of the donor rather than effecting any real form of solidarity and was discordant with such solidarity.

Within the *Oppression Model*, the involvement of formal carers again has its basis in a form of generosity that is not centred on the virtues of civic society. If it was, marginalisation of people with intellectual disabilities and arbitrary denial of their human rights would no longer be an issue. The emergence of service-based rights commissions and of national advocacy groups is evidence of their continuation, albeit in more attractive guises. No one doubts the intentionality of goodwill that underpins the work of carers (including this writer) but, as long as that goodwill is directed solely towards the provision of care/service for *disabled* individuals, it will maintain those individuals in their states of *disability*. Thus, the *status quo* is protected, with generations of carers and service personnel metaphorically reaping the good things of life on the backs of those, on whose disablement their comforts depend (Freire, 1996; Sobrino, 2008). Furthermore, the operation of service-based rights commissions and advocacy groups may be viewed as further examples of goodwill intentionality which may be fundamentally compromised by their existence within the context of an *Oppression Model* of service.

Professions within intellectual disability services have justified their existence on the basis that they provide a specialist service to a specific group of people (Northway et al., 2006). The image that emerges of service, and of its place in society, is one in which the failure of mainstream society to address the individualised health, social and educational needs of people with intellectual impairment has led to the predetermined failure (jeopardy) of these people to achieve mainstream societal norms in those and related regards. Bereft of any real leadership, such models of service were directed and managed in a largely hierarchical and authoritarian manner, with limited autonomy being afforded those who worked at the interface between service provider and service recipient.

Institutions and Services: Waxing and Waning of Power

When the Universal Declaration of Human Rights was launched in 1948, in response to the human rights violations which had been perpetrated during the Second World War, it was hoped that this would lead to an increased awareness of the realities of those who had been marginalised. This was not, however, the case, and further civil rights movements arose in the 1950s and 1960s focused on ethnic racism and physical disability.

Similar unease began to develop among the families and friends of people with intellectual impairments who, in the light of emerging evidence from social science, began to demand better outcomes for their loved ones. Spurred on by new social perspectives from Scandinavian countries, the normalisation movement grew, with a focus on human services, geared towards providing patterns of life more akin to those of mainstream society (Wolfensberger, 1972). In the United States and Canada, this led to the gradual movement of service away from authoritarian 'hospital' models and towards more disseminated 'community' ones, with a less hierarchical, flatter management structure. Similar developments took place some years afterwards in the United Kingdom (Audit Commission, 1992) but considerably later in Ireland (Health Service Executive, 2011). These changes allowed intellectual impairment and related disability to be examined through different lenses, facilitating a reassessment of the oppressive realities of historic service provision and the human realities of the people who had experienced such services.

This also meant that many service staff were required to reflect on the roles that they had hitherto unwittingly played in the lives of these people; perpetuating, what Wolfensberger (1972) called the 'wasting' of people's lives. Some of the service staff, however, who emerged from this process of self-examination, became key advocates for people with intellectual impairment and visionary leaders, amongst them Wolf Wolfensberger, John O'Brien, Jim Mansell and Michael Kendrick, making contributions far beyond the confines of their own services or countries. Despite this, though, traditional service models have persisted, whether in the form of modified institutions or as institutional approaches in smaller community settings. Sadly, a number of such services have been the focus of very public scandals which have exposed their lack of leadership.

Three Countries. Three Services. Three Failures in Leadership

Over the past few years, three significant and very public manifestations of care erosion have emerged in the United States of America, the United Kingdom and the Republic of Ireland. While each of these has been documented in reports and media elsewhere, it is useful to briefly recap on the main details. The events within the Oswald D. Heck Developmental Centre included widespread neglect and abuse of people, non-response to parental concerns and lack of leadership, culminating in the death of a young boy, Jonathan Carey, who was asphyxiated while under the supervision of two care workers (New York State Inspector General, 2008; Hakim, 2011). Subsequent reviews of the New York State systems for 'vulnerable persons' highlighted significant inadequacies (Sundram, 2011).

The events in Áras Attracta (Ireland) and Winterbourne View (UK) were the subject of investigative journalism, captured by hidden cameras, and broadcast via television documentaries. The most recent of these, *Inside Bungalow 3* (RTÉ Investigations Unit, 2014) provided graphic video of three older women, who could not verbally communicate, being shouted at, threatened and slapped by care workers from a variety of professional backgrounds. The documentary also demonstrated a living environment marked by dehumanisation, in which the women appeared to have been objectified, and a marked lack of care or interest. It is clear that the three women actually had significant abilities for non-verbal communication and that these were ignored or unrecognised; they were met instead with restrictive practices. It was noted that in the care setting that was the subject of the documentary, many staff either partook in the above practices or failed to intervene.

A similar picture was presented by BBC Panorama in *Undercover Care: The Abuse Uncovered* (BBC Panorama, 2011). Again, a group of care workers from various backgrounds, including health and social care professionals, subjected men and women with intellectual disabilities, autism and mental health concerns to what might be described as systematic abuse. The reports that followed each of the above scandals all point to the failure or absence of leadership at various levels (Sundram, 2011; Department of Health, 2012; Mencap, 2014; Áras Attracta Swinford Review Group, 2016a, 2016b) and called for the development of such leadership at all levels, including, and this is particularly important, within those who avail of services. The ability to achieve this is, however, potentially impaired by the increasing demand for risk management and safeguarding within health, education and social services, grounded in the concept of vulnerability and the imposition of service standards.

Recreating Disability: Vulnerability and Control

Western society has become increasingly litigious and this has resulted in a growing focus on the minimisation of risk. Thus, there is within organisations a constant fear that an action or inaction may lead to an outcome that will have a financial or reputational implication for the organisation. This is particularly so where that organisation is a provider of services to people who may be categorised as 'vulnerable'. The occurrence of scandals, such as those mentioned above, has fed into the designation of people who experience intellectual disability as 'vulnerable'. Indeed, within Ireland, this has now been formalised in the statutes in the form of the *National Vetting Bureau (Children and Vulnerable Adults) Act* (Government of Ireland, 2010). While this writer does not deny that some people are vulnerable (whether or not they experience intellectual disabilities), it appears that approaches such as this are congregational and stereotyping in nature. They serve to re-create disability; once the label of vulnerability is applied, it starts a process whereby they can be deprived of normative living and relationships. Furthermore, they will often be excluded from those higher value systems which have been premised on high levels of competence and cognitive function. The outcome is often one of material and experiential poverty, powerlessness and submission.

An example of how such labelling can affect people was witnessed by the writer. While he was working in a university which provided an inclusive education programme for people who experience intellectual disability, a policy was introduced which stated that all people who engaged with students on that programme were required to be vetted by the local police. This was in line with the aforementioned *National Vetting Bureau (Children and Vulnerable Adults) Act*. The consequences were widespread. Firstly, these were the only adult students in the college to be designated as 'vulnerable' and this was solely on the basis of them 'having an intellectual disability'. Secondly, it meant that all academics, administrators and other students who engaged with them were required to be vetted, compromising peer-relationships, stymying social inclusion and recreating service-style relationships. Such risk-driven approaches arguably re-create and re-enforce margins at the edge of society. Sherwin (2010) referred to the fact that having managed to work through problems within individuals which prevented them from achieving their potentials, we are now struggling to address the structural barriers. As is clear from the two television documentaries, such structural issues are creating situations whereby the margin is controlled, and often staffed by individuals who are not adequately prepared for the complex nature of engagement that is required in human services. This poses a significant challenge for leadership in such services.

Challenges for Leadership in Service Provision

Vulnerability legislation, along with the focus on risk management, has become embedded in policy, with standards being elucidated and overseen by bodies such as the Care Quality Commission in the UK and the Health Information and Quality Authority (HIQA) in Ireland. Announced and unannounced inspections are now being routinely carried out by these bodies and they wield significant clout, with the power to close service settings if standards are not being met. Concurrently, policies of de-congregation and movement to community-based living continue to be enacted (HSE, 2011), with an increasing focus on independent living. In Ireland, this has been a belated process, and a traumatic one for all parties, with service management often facing with impossible scenarios whereby the health service policy of de-congregation is being enforced at the same time as the standards authority is threatening closure; which policy takes precedence? That of the health service, which can stop service funding, or that of the standards authority, which can close the service down?

This situation is paralysing for services and greatly reduces the potential for real leadership to occur. The result is that many services for people who experience intellectual disability find themselves operating either in, or on the verge of, crisis (See Figure 1.1), with the potential for real leadership stymied by the need for compliance with policy and standards. Instead, the focus of senior management, middle management and care providers becomes one of avoiding/managing the crisis situation, fulfilling the criteria set by the funding and

	Compliance with standards Compliance with governance for funding	
Senior Management (SM)	Requirement to demonstrate compliance with standards Requirement to comply with funding conditions Requirement to provide service governance *(management – not leadership)*	Deterioration of Top-Level Leadership
Middle Management (MM)	Requirement to demonstrate compliance to SM Requirement to daily manage service provision *(management - not leadership)*	Deterioration of Mid-Level Leadership
Unit Staff	Requirement to demonstrate compliance to SM/MM Requirement to provide direct service to residents *(management - not care)*	Standards of Care Reduce
Service Residents	Lack of individualised, person-outcome directed service Reduced standards of service *(basic management – care erosion)*	Increased Risk for Service Residents
Families	Stress, fear, distress, powerless Distrust of management and staff *(exclusion – not family support)*	Alienation

Figure 1.1 Challenges to leadership in the context of policy and standards compliance.

monitoring bodies. The outcome is that neither policy nor standards are adequately met and the real risk of care erosion results. The provision of human service to people who experience intellectual disability falls by the wayside, with them becoming objectified and similarly 'managed', setting the scene for scenarios such as those in *Áras Attracta*, Winterbourne View and the Oswald D. Heck Developmental Centre.

Conclusion

It has been shown that services have developed along a trajectory which has seen significant improvements for people who experience intellectual disability. There has been a greater focus on human rights, largely supported by the widespread ratification of the United Nations Convention on the Rights of Persons with Disabilities (UN, 2006). Many people have seen their living conditions improve, with greater personal space and more opportunities for normative lives. However, the paternalism of the past is ever threatening to influence the provision of services and to curtail those opportunities. The frequency of reports into poor standards and occurrence of abuse in service suggests that many challenges remain and that some have not experienced those significant improvements in their lives. There is a need for new leadership approaches within health, education and social services (Broderick, 2017) to address such shortcomings and guide the development of new, inclusive and participatory models of human services, which focus on supporting individuals to achieve lives of opportunity. Indeed, Jukes and Aspinall (2015) have indicated that such leadership is crucial if intellectual disability services are to be transformed into human services that are directed towards the fulfilment of person-centred outcomes (Department of Health, 2012).

Key Concepts Discussed

■ Consideration of the contextual backdrop where health, educational and social services for people with an intellectual disability became centred on single sites in exclusive settings, with people *managed*, leaving limited scope for leadership.
■ The importance of facilitating leadership to emerge in models of service provision, based on partnership and empowerment. The role of families and others in making sure that the voice of people with intellectual disabilities was heard.
■ Exploration of three examples where lack of leadership impacted very significantly on people receiving service: a) Áras Attracta; b) Winterborne View; c) Oswald D. Heck.
■ The emerging challenges to leadership in the light of requirements to comply with standards and policy.
■ How new models of shared-leadership are required to ensure that people with intellectual disabilities are empowered to live the lives of their own choosing.

Key Readings on Leadership in Intellectual Disability Service

■ Áras Attracta Swinford Review Group (2016a). *Time for Action: Priority Actions Arising from National Consultation*. Dublin: Health Service Executive. This report addresses the wider system of service provision for people with a disability in Ireland and proposes a range of actions including 55 priority actions that emerged from a national process of consultation with stakeholders involved in disability services and the wider public.
■ Áras Attracta Swinford Review Group (2016b). *What Matters Most*. Dublin: Health Service Executive. This report sets out the findings of the Review Group in relation to Áras Attracta itself. It includes recommendations relating to Áras

Attracta management, actions for the HSE at a national level and a 'road map' to guide all managers of congregated settings as they move towards de-congregation.

■ Department of Health (2012). *Transforming Care: A National Response to Winterbourne View Hospital.* London: Department of Health. This report presents the UK government's final response to the events at Winterbourne View hospital. It sets out a programme of action to transform services for people with learning disabilities or autism and mental health conditions or behaviours described as challenging.

■ Jukes, M. (2013). *Practice Leadership in Mental Health and Intellectual Disability Nursing.* London: Quay Books. This book explores challenges to clinical practice leadership in intellectual disability and mental health nursing in the UK, providing suggestions as to how leadership in practice can be improved.

Useful Websites

■ American Association on Intellectual and Developmental Disabilities https://aaidd.org/.
■ British Institute of Learning Disabilities (BILD) http://www.bild.org.uk/
■ Inclusion Europe http://inclusion-europe.eu/
■ Inclusion Ireland http://www.inclusionireland.ie/
■ MENCAP https://www.mencap.org.uk/

References

Áras Attracta Swinford Review Group (2016a). *Time for Action: Priority Actions Arising from National Consultation.* Dublin: Health Service Executive.

Áras Attracta Swinford Review Group (2016b). *What Matters Most.* Dublin: Health Service Executive.

Audit Commission (1992). *The Community Revolution: Personal Social Services and Community Care*. London: HMSO.

BBC (2011). *Undercover Care: The Abuse Uncovered*. London: BBC Panorama. BBC One. 31 May 2011.

Brandon, M. (1957). The intellectual and social status of children of mental defectives. *Journal of Mental Science* 103, 710–738.

Broderick, B. (2017). Optimising leadership within the intellectual disability service delivery system. *Frontline* 106. Online: Available at: https://frontline-ireland.com/optimising-leadership-within-intellectual-disability-service-delivery-system. Accessed 21 June 2018.

Brunwasser, M. (2010). Unlikely allies in Bulgaria reveal fatal mental health neglect. *New York Times* October 5. Online: Available at: https://www.nytimes.com/2010/10/06/world/europe/06bulgaria.html?pagewanted=2&sq=Bulgaria&st=cse&scp=2. Accessed 15 June 2018.

Department of Health (2012). *Transforming Care: A National Response to Winterbourne View Hospital*. London: Department of Health.

Freire, P. (1996). *Pedagogy of the Oppressed*. London: Penguin Books.

Giddens, A. (2009). *Sociology*. (6th ed.) Cambridge: Polity Press.

Goffman, E. (1961). *Asylums*. London: Penguin Books.

Government of Ireland (2010). *National Vetting Bureau (Children and Vulnerable Adults) Act 2010*. Dublin: The Stationery Office.

Gribben, J. (1993). *In Search of the Double Helix*. London: Black Swan.

Hakim, D. (2011). A disabled boy's death, and a system in disarray. *The New York Times* June 5. Online: Available at: https://www.nytimes.com/2011/06/06/nyregion/boys-death-highlights-crisis-in-homes-for-disabled.html. Accessed 18 April 2018.

Health Service Executive (2011). *Time to Move on from Congregated Settings*. Dublin: HSE.

Jukes, M. and Aspinall, S. (2015). Leadership and learning disability nursing. *British Journal of Nursing* 24(18), 912–916.

Mencap (2014). *Out of Sight: Stopping the Neglect and Abuse of People with a Learning Disability*. London: Mencap.

Metzler, I. (2016). *Fools and Idiots? Intellectual Disability in the Middle Ages*. Manchester: Manchester University Press.

Mitch, D. (2018). The role of education and skill in the British industrial revolution. In: J. Mokyr (Ed.) *The British Industrial Revolution*. New York: Routledge. pp. 241–279.

New York State Inspector General (2008). *A Critical Examination of State Agency Investigations into Allegations of Abuse of Jonathan Carey*. New York: Office of the Inspector General.

Northway, R., Hutchinson, C. and Kingdon, A. (Eds.) (2006). *Shaping the Future: A Vision for Learning Disability Nursing*. United Kingdom: UK Learning Disability Consultant Nurse Network.

Ntinas, K. (2007). Behavior modification and the principle of normalization: Clash or synthesis? *Behavioural Interventions 22*, 165–177.

Priestley, M. (1999). *Disability Politics and Community Care*. London: Jessica Kingsley.

Rafter, N. (1992). Claims-making and socio-cultural context in the first U.S. eugenics campaign. *Social Problems 39*(1), 17–34.

Reilly, P. (2015). Eugenics and involuntary sterilization: 1907–2015. *Annual Review of Genomics and Human Genetics 16*, 351–368.

Robins, J. (1986). *Fools and Mad*. Dublin: Institute of Public Administration.

RTE Investigations Unit (2014) *Inside Bungalow 3*. Dublin: RTE Prime Time Investigates. Online: Available at: https://www.rte .ie/news/player/prime-time-web/2014/1209/. Accessed 18 April 2018.

Sheerin, F. (1998). Marginalisation in learning disability services: An exploration of the issues. *Nursing Review 16*(3/4), 70–73.

Sheerin, F. (2013a). Jesus and the portrayal of people with disabilities in the scriptures. *Spiritan Horizons 8*, 61–71.

Sheerin, F. (2013b). Intellectual disability in Ireland: Changing perspectives. *Frontline 90*. Online: Available at: https://frontline-ir eland.com/intellectual-disability-in-ireland-changing-perspectives. Accessed 15 June 2018.

Sheerin, F., Keenan, P. and Lawler, D. (2013). Mothers with intellectual disabilities: Interactions with children and family services in Ireland. *British Journal of Learning Disabilities 41*, 189–196.

Sheerin, F. and Sines, D. (1999). Marginalization and its effects on the sexuality- related potentials of the learning disabled person. *Journal of Intellectual Disabilities 3*(1), 39–49.

Sherwin, J. (2010). Leadership for social inclusion in the lives of people with disabilities. *The International Journal of Leadership in Public Services 6* supp., 84–93.

Sobrino, J. (2008) *The Eye of the Needle: No Salvation Outside the Poor*. London: Darton, Longman and Todd.

Sundram, C. (2011). *The Measure of a Society: Protection of Vulnerable Persons in Residential Facilities Against Abuse & Neglect*. Report submitted to Governor Andrew M. Cuomo. Online: Available at: https://www.governor.ny.gov/sites/govern or.ny.gov/files/archive/assets/documents/justice4specialneeds. pdf. Accessed 16 June 2018.

Taskforce on Active Citizenship (2007). *The Concept of Active Citizenship*. Dublin: Taskforce on Active Citizenship.

United Nations (2006). *Convention on the Rights of Persons with Disabilities*. Geneva: United Nations.

United Nations (2010). *Monitoring the Convention on the Rights of Persons with Disabilities*. Geneva: United Nations.

Wolfensberger, W. (1972). *The Principle of Normalization in Human Services*. Toronto: National Institute on Mental Retardation.

Worsley, P. (1992). *Introducing Sociology*. London: Penguin.

Wright, D. (2000). Learning disability and the New Poor Law in England, 1834–1867. *Disability and Society 15*(5), 731–745.

Young, I. (1990). *Justice and the Politics of Difference*. Princeton, NJ: Princeton University Press.

Chapter 2

Moving Models: Leading Through Constant Change

Ruth Northway

Contents

Chapter Topics

- **How models of service provision for people who experience intellectual disabilities have changed over the past 50 years**
- **The key drivers that gave rise to these changes and their impact on leadership**
- **The current context and the implications for future leadership models**

Introduction

The focus within this chapter is primarily on changes that have happened to services and supports for people who experience intellectual disabilities over the past 50 years and the implications of these for leadership. Nonetheless, a quick look at any historical account of how society has understood the group of people currently referred to as experiencing intellectual disabilities will reveal that such changes have been occurring for many centuries. New models and approaches have emerged at many different points, each one offering the promise of new and better things. Progress has been made and yet change is still needed. Change does not, however, simply happen and often it is poorly managed even where it is desperately needed. Many factors have influenced the extent to which the promise of positive change has been realised and one of these factors is the presence or absence of effective leadership.

Moving Models

The major change in services and supports for people who experience intellectual disabilities that has occurred in many countries is the move from large-scale institutional provision to smaller-scale community-based patterns of support. This change has been driven by a range of factors of which three will be explored here: understandings of the nature of intellectual disability, evidence of poor standards of care and a changing value base. While they are explored separately here it must be understood that they are interdependent with change in one area leading to development in another, rather than three parallel strands of influence.

Understandings of Intellectual Disability

What we currently understand and refer to as 'intellectual disability' has changed significantly over time and even today a range of understandings is evident across countries and cultures. However, what is constant is that how intellectual disability is defined and understood shapes the nature of services and supports that are provided. Indeed, Williams and Tyne (1988) argue that while as individual citizens we may value those who experience intellectual disabilities as friends, neighbours and colleagues, wider societal views have often been negative and it is these social values that influence service development and delivery. For example, Wolfensberger (1992) identified a number of common negative social roles into which people with intellectual disabilities have been cast: as 'other', as non-human, as a menace, as an object of ridicule, as an object of pity, as a burden of charity, as a child, as a diseased organism and as dead or dying. These varying understandings of intellectual disability have had a direct influence on service development and delivery as will be seen in the paragraphs below.

When large-scale institutions for people who experience intellectual disabilities were developed in the mid and late 19th century they were originally intended to have an educational function. People who experience intellectual disabilities were viewed as requiring specific education in order to develop the skills they needed to function in a society that was becoming increasingly industrialised. However, when progress was not achieved and economic constraints within institutions became more challenging, the lack of progress was attributed to a failure on the part of people who experience intellectual disabilities to learn rather than to a service that failed to provide appropriate support (Ryan and Thomas, 1987). In subsequent years, the focus thus shifted to a medicalised pattern of service provision with intellectual disability being viewed as a medical 'problem' and the institutions were viewed as places of treatment and containment protecting not only those who resided within them but also wider society for whom people who experience intellectual disabilities were viewed as a threat to the social, genetic and moral fabric of society.

As will be seen in the next section, however, over time it became evident that conditions within such long stay institutions were poor and not acceptable. Alongside this came a reassessment of how the nature of intellectual disability should be understood and, rather than viewing it as a medical problem located within the individual that needed to be treated or 'cured', thinking shifted to viewing it more as a social issue. This took two forms.

First, in the wider context of disability, the view of disability as an individual or medical 'problem' began to be challenged. Organisations of disabled people advocated that rather than someone being disabled by their impairment they were in fact disabled by a range of social, physical, economic and attitudinal barriers that prevent their full inclusion in society (Oliver, 1996). Chappell (1997) argued that this social model of disability had a limited impact within the context of intellectual disabilities and others (for example Crow, 1996) have critiqued this conceptualisation of disability arguing that even if all barriers to participation were removed impairment would still have a substantial limiting effect on the day to day lives of individuals. However, the importance of removing barriers to participation has gained traction within policy and practice for people who experience intellectual disabilities and an example of this can be seen in the requirement to make reasonable adjustments to ensure equal access to goods and services as set out by the Equalities Act 2010 in England and Wales.

The second impact of viewing intellectual disability as a social rather than a medical issue was that it led to a changing model of service provision. If intellectual disability is viewed as a social rather than a medical issue, then it logically follows that a pattern of services based on long stay hospital/institutional provision staffed primarily by nurses and doctors is not appropriate. What emerged, therefore, in the late 1970s and early 1980s was a social model of care that sought to support people in their own communities through a system of community-based services. The process of deinstitutionalisation therefore began.

The rate of deinstitutionalisation has varied between countries and in some places, institutions still exist in the absence of community-based supports. However, in many countries, a system of supported living, community-based day provision and employment and community-based professional support has developed alongside moves to support the inclusion of people who experience intellectual disabilities in educational, residential and health services available within their communities.

Questionable Standards

As was noted above concerns were raised regarding standards of care within long stay institutions. Within the UK the first major inquiry into standards of care was the Ely Inquiry published in 1969 (Howe et al., 1969). This inquiry was launched after allegations of poor care within Ely Hospital in Cardiff were published in the *News of the World* newspaper. What emerged was that a member of staff at the hospital had raised concerns both internally in the hospital and externally to the health authority but no actions had been taken. They had therefore then approached the newspaper which published the allegations of cruelty, inhumane treatment, theft and a lack of appropriate medical care. The inquiry was held in private but the findings were published and led to the 1970 White Paper 'Better Services for the Mentally Handicapped' which set out a programme of improvement for conditions within long stay institutions, a reduction in hospital provision and the development of community-based services and support.

The Ely Inquiry was not, however, an isolated example of poor care within long stay institutions. Other inquiries followed within the UK (Ryan and Thomas, 1987) and in other countries. Within the USA Blatt and Kaplan (1966) published their seminal series of photographs titled 'Christmas in Purgatory'. This series of black and white photographs set out the stark reality of living conditions endured by people who experience intellectual disabilities within long stay institutions in the United States and when some of these photos appeared in an edition of *Life Magazine* these conditions were revealed to the general public just as the newspaper story had done in the UK. Wehmeyer and Schalock (2013) note that this focused public attention on such institutions within their communities, and one journalist called Geraldo Rivera focused in particular on the Willowbrook State Hospital. Rivera's *exposé* identified people living in overcrowded and unsanitary conditions; some had experienced years of maltreatment leading to physical impairments and most were either partially clothed or unclothed (Wehmeyer and Schalock, 2013). The documentary produced by Rivera was aired in 1972 and led to 'civil outrage if not unrest' (Wehmeyer and Schalock, 2013: 224). The hospital finally closed in 1987, perhaps indicating that even where standards of care are poor, effecting change can be a long process.

It was to be hoped that the move towards community-based supports and models of care would both improve standards and end poor, abusive and neglectful treatment. Indeed, the life opportunities of many people who experience intellectual disabilities now are much improved. However, experience has shown that simply closing long stay institutions does not automatically end poor and abusive care.

Since the Ely Inquiry and the exposure of standards of care at Willowbrook a number of examples of poor care, abuse and neglect have continued to be exposed within community-based and smaller-scale facilities. For example, in in the UK in the early 1990s reports of wide-scale abuse at two residential homes in Buckinghamshire emerged leading to an independent inquiry and criminal prosecutions but also leading to enduring negative impact on many of the residents who had been living there (Pring, 2011).

In 2011, in a sequence of events depressingly similar to those leading to the Ely Inquiry (concerns being raised both internally in the organisation and externally with no action before reporting to the media) the documentary programme *Panorama* (BBC, 2011) aired the findings of an undercover investigation of abuse within Winterbourne View, a privately run assessment and treatment unit. This service was commissioned to offer 'specialist' treatment and assessment facilities for those with complex behavioural support needs. Such placements were high cost and often meant that those who were patients there were geographically isolated from family and support networks having travelled a distance to receive this 'specialist' support. What emerged in the documentary, however, was the abusive and neglectful nature of care received by some of those who were resident within the unit. A serious case review followed (Flynn, 2012), 11 staff were eventually prosecuted with six receiving custodial sentences.

Such examples, however, have not been confined to the UK. In December 2014 RTÉ, in their *Prime Time Investigates* programme (RTÉ Investigations Unit, 2014), aired a documentary detailing a similar undercover investigation to that undertaken in Winterbourne View. This time, however, the focus was on standards of care within Bungalow 3 in the Áras Attracta Service. This campus-based service had opened in 1988 when it received residents transferred following the closure of a long stay institution. Following the documentary, a review group was formed with the terms of reference being agreed in January 2015 and the report being published in 2016 (Áras Attracta Swinford Review Group, 2016). The review concluded that the daily lives of those resident within the unit resulted in a poor quality of life and that one of the contributing factors was a lack of leadership within the service. Changes were identified as being required at both service and national level to effect the change required to ensure a rights-based social model of care delivery. At a service level, the need to strengthen and enhance leadership and management was recommended while at a national level the need to develop a leadership development programme including the management of change for managers within all congregated settings was identified. It was further noted that transitioning service provision to a community-based approach requires a change in culture and that this, in turn, highlights the need to:

> Identify leaders at all levels in the organisation who are ready, willing and able to lead the change.
>
> **(Áras Attracta Swinford Review Group, 2016: 16)**

The absence of effective leadership is thus viewed as a key element of poor and abusive care while also being identified as a required element to effect positive change.

Changing Values

Jackson (2016) has argued that when we examine the changes that have taken place in the context of intellectual disabilities we also need to explore the ideologies and beliefs that underpin such developments. Accordingly, some key factors that have influenced and driven change over the past 50 years will be considered, namely normalisation, human rights and advocacy.

Cummins (2016) identifies six stages in the development of intellectual disability services of which 'normalisation' is stage five. The origins of normalisation lie in Scandinavia in the 1960s where in Denmark the 1959 Retardation Act sought to promote an existence for people who experience intellectual disabilities 'as close to normal living conditions as possible' (Bank-Mikkelson, 1980: 56). This approach was then developed by pioneers such as Bank-Mikkelson (1980) in Denmark and Nirje (1969) in Sweden. Based on the principle that people who experience intellectual disabilities should have the same rights as others to normal patterns of life within their communities, normalisation influenced both policy and service development. It also informed developments elsewhere such as the All Wales Strategy (Welsh Office, 1983) within the UK.

In North America, Wolfensberger (1972) developed normalisation (later renamed social role valorisation [Wolfensberger, 1992]) in a manner that differed from the Scandinavian approach in two key ways (Emerson, 1992). First, it placed an emphasis on how disadvantaged people (such as those who experience intellectual disabilities) are portrayed to and viewed by wider society. Second, it reformulated the aims to focus on the creation of socially valued roles rather than on promoting the right to patterns of life that are culturally normative (Emerson, 1992).

Normalisation had a significant impact internationally on service development not just in terms of institutional closure but also in terms of the nature of community-based supports that were developed to enable people to remain and be supported within their communities. However, while its principles were promoted in many places with 'evangelical fervour' (Cummins, 2016: 49) it was also interpreted in many different ways. Jackson (2011) notes that normalisation is an ideology and that some difficulties arose in its translation into practice. He further argues that ideologies should act as a guide to thought and action but not dictate practice. During the 1990s, therefore, while acknowledging the tremendous impact that normalisation had on the development of services and supports for people who experience intellectual disabilities, critiques also started to emerge (see for example those in the edited book by Brown and Smith, 1992).

Early versions of normalisation had a specific focus on the promotion of equal rights. The Universal Declaration of Human Rights (United Nations, 1948) had previously set out a range of rights to which all persons (including those with disabilities) should have access and placed responsibility on states to ensure that such rights were realised. However, while all of these rights should equally apply to disabled people there was a growing realisation that additional protections needed to be in place and hence in 2006 the Convention on the Rights of Persons with Disabilities (UN, 2006) was published. Setting out a range of rights, this document was based on the principles of respect for autonomy, difference, dignity, equality of opportunity, inclusion and non-discrimination. Mechanisms were also established to monitor implementation of the Convention. Alongside such international developments, individual countries also enacted disability rights legislation such as the Americans with Disabilities Act (1990) and the Disability Discrimination Act (2005) in the United Kingdom.

While the focus of such developments was broadly on disabled persons rather than specifically on people who experience intellectual disabilities they were included within these provisions and the rights agenda has impacted on the development of services and supports in the field of intellectual disability. For example, the concept of 'reasonable adjustments' promoted within the UK Equality Act (2010) means that people who experience intellectual disabilities now have the right to expect adjustments to be made to the way services are provided in order to ensure that they can access such services on an equal level to other citizens. Such adjustments include the provision of information in accessible formats, providing additional time for healthcare appointments and the provision of additional supports. However, while legislation and policy can play an important role in ensuring that the rights of people who experience intellectual disabilities are protected, issues can arise in their translation into practice. In such circumstances, advocacy can have an important role to play in ensuring that rights are upheld, and injustices are addressed.

When advocacy is referred to in the context of intellectual disabilities, the focus is usually on self-advocacy by people who experience intellectual disabilities. However, it has been suggested that there have been three 'waves' in the disability movement, the first of which was professional domination which dominated until the mid-20th century; the second wave emerged in the 1950s and was led by parents; followed by the third wave of self-advocacy that began to exert an influence from the mid-1970s (Ferguson et al., 2013). It is thus evident that advocacy for service improvement initially came from parents who questioned the nature of professional services that were being provided for them and their children (Wehmeyer and Schalock, 2013). In more recent years, however, people who experience intellectual disabilities have themselves sought to raise awareness of their rights and needs through self-advocacy. While self-advocacy can encompass many different activities, its key features include people with intellectual disabilities having a voice, being listened to, taking control over their own lives and working with others to effect changes in their communities (Inclusion International, 2016). It is in differing stages of development in different parts of the world and requires better and more effective supports in many areas. Nonetheless, it is now a global movement seeking to promote the inclusion of people who experience intellectual disabilities (Inclusion International, 2016).

Understanding the Current Context

As has been seen, many changes have taken place in the context of intellectual disability services over the past 50 years. Nonetheless, while service improvements have been achieved much remains to be done: even when we know what changes are required the pace of change may be slow (Northway, 2018a). Moreover, 'best practice' is often not universal; as has been seen earlier in this chapter examples of poor practice, abuse and neglect continue to emerge, and calls for leadership to be more effective and strengthened remain (Áras Attracta Swinford Review Group, 2016). It is therefore important to consider the factors that are currently impacting on the provision of services and supports to determine the nature of leadership required in the future.

At any given point in history, there is evidence of both historical patterns or models of service provision and new and emerging approaches. However, in the early decades of the 21st century in many countries large-scale institutional provision has closed, and in its place a more diverse and dispersed pattern of support is evident. While this approach seeks to support people who experience intellectual disabilities in their own communities and to promote inclusion, it presents some challenges in relation to leadership. Within institutions, top-down models of bureaucratic managerial control dominated but in community-based support staff are more often working in either small teams or on their own, meaning that managerial support is often more remote. In addition, direct care positions are often low paid and hence there can be frequent changes of staff, provision of training can be challenging and previous experience of supporting people with intellectual disabilities can be minimal or non-existent. Within this context, previous leadership approaches may not be appropriate: a point that will be returned to later in this chapter.

Within large-scale institutional services, people who experience intellectual disabilities were often subjected to depersonalised treatment with rigid and fixed regimes that offered little opportunity for individualised supports. The move to more community-based models of care and support has sought to promote a more individualised and person-centred approach in which the personal priorities and wishes of the individual who experiences intellectual disabilities provides the starting point rather than the needs of the organisation. As with any change of approach, there can be a gap between rhetoric and reality, and person-centred approaches to support are not universally evident. However, it can be seen that moves towards this present different challenges for leadership since traditional power structures are challenged and those who are supported by a service move towards greater leadership and control of their own lives.

A further challenge to leadership arising from changing models of care is that increasingly support is provided by a range of different professionals and agencies, each with their own values, priorities, budgets and policies. While many of these organisational characteristics may be shared or complementary, in other cases they may differ, and hence leaders need to be able to work across traditional organisational boundaries and understand different organisational cultures. This also means that leadership may be needed from those who are not in what have previously been considered leadership roles and at a range of different levels within organisations.

Perhaps one of the greatest challenges to leadership within current models of care is that posed by rising levels of need for support at a time of increasing financial constraints. Jackson (2011) predicted that the global financial recession would present a significant challenge in terms of providing high-quality supports for people who experience intellectual disabilities, and there is evidence that financial constraints are having such an impact. One of the worrying features of the current situation is that limited resources appear to be leading to services focusing primarily on those with the most immediate need for support meaning that preventative and early intervention services are being reduced. While there is some logic to such prioritisation it may eventually lead to higher long-term costs and the human costs of not receiving support until crisis point is reached are of considerable concern

(Northway, 2018b). Limited financial resources also present specific leadership challenges as services seek to improve (or at least maintain) quality.

Leadership for the Future

In times of change leaders are needed, but changing times and situations mean that not only do models of care and support change but also that approaches to leadership need to be examined and critically assessed for their utility in the new context. As has been previously noted within institutional service provision, traditional hierarchical models of bureaucratic management dominated, with power and control being largely vested in the medical profession. Such models have limited usefulness within current models of care and support, and hence alternative approaches need to be explored.

Weberg (2012) suggests that traditional leadership approaches have focused on the traits or characteristics of leaders, the situations in which leaders operate and the interaction between these two factors. This, he argues, has led to linear thinking, a lack of awareness of organisational culture and a lack of preparedness for innovation. However, he suggests that evidence of increasing costs and poor outcomes suggests that such leadership approaches are outdated. While he focuses specifically on healthcare organisations, the issues highlighted in the previous section of this chapter (particularly the failures in care) suggest that the same may also be true in relation to current models of support for people who experience intellectual disabilities.

Clarke (2018) argues that there are three key challenges that a new model of leadership needs to address – the challenge of leadership capacity, the challenge of context and the challenge of responsibility. Each of these will be examined in turn in relation to current services and supports for people who experience intellectual disabilities.

Clarke (2018) suggests that when the question of *leadership capacity* is examined, the thinking tends to focus on whether there are people within the organisation to fill formal leadership roles. However, he argues for a relational approach to leadership in which the skills and strengths of all within the organisation are viewed as a 'huge reservoir of untapped leadership talent' (ibid. 5). Within the context of dispersed community-based services in intellectual disabilities, this opens up space for leadership to be developed at a range of different levels. This is important since within community-based services staff are frequently working without direct managerial supervision and there is a need to identify leaders at all levels who have the willingness and capacity to lead change (Áras Attracta Swinford Review Group, 2016). Most importantly, it also means that leadership by people who experience intellectual disabilities themselves along with their families and friends can be recognised. Nonetheless, it remains important to enable people to grow into leadership roles through the provision of appropriate support and development opportunities. This is also important for people who experience intellectual disabilities themselves where such development opportunities may be limited (Caldwell, 2010).

According to Clarke (2018), there is increasing research which indicates that *context* influences whether particular leadership approaches are effective. As has been noted above, the models of care that are now developing in intellectual disability services are doing so in a context that is both changing and increasingly complex. Weberg (2012) attributes leadership failure in complex contexts to factors such as linear thinking and a lack of understanding of organisational culture. If leadership is thus to be an answer to some of the failures in care recently highlighted, (Áras Attracta Swinford Review, 2016) thinking needs to shift to a more systems-based relational approach that understands and seeks to positively influence organisational cultures. Such an approach requires leaders to recognise that they are part of the system and to use their position to shape developments through their interactions with both the formal and informal cultures within the organisation (Weberg, 2012).

The third leadership challenge identified by Clarke (2018) is the *challenge of responsibility*, which is related to the current public crisis of confidence in business arising from financial scandals and poor performance. However, as this chapter has demonstrated, the history of services that support people who experience intellectual disabilities has a recurring theme of inquiries into poor standards of care and abuse leading to public outcries and calls for change. It would thus seem that the challenge of responsibility is one which leaders in intellectual disability services also need to address. Clarke (2018) argues that traditionally ethical behaviour has often been viewed as something to be imposed in a hierarchical manner. Even where this is well intentioned, he argues, the impact of such an approach may be limited, suggesting that a more effective approach may be to think about ethical behaviour as being developed through the interactions between leaders and followers. This would appear particularly pertinent in the context of increasingly dispersed models of intellectual disability service, where individual staff members may be working relatively independently and thus need to have the capacity to uphold ethical standards in their day to day work without direct supervision.

For Clarke (2018), leadership is about relationships, which seems fitting in current models of care and support for people who experience intellectual disabilities, where the focus is on person-centred approaches, rights and inclusion: relationships are fundamental to each of these areas. He also argues that this shared approach to leadership means that it is not fixed within rigid structures but rather that it emerges in keeping with needs and complexity. Given the past and current challenges explored in earlier sections of this chapter, such an approach seems promising as we look to the future.

Conclusion

This chapter has explored the history of models of care and support for people who experience intellectual disabilities and their families over the past 50 years. While services have developed differently in different countries, some recurring themes have been identified. The challenges currently facing services have also been considered and the implications for leadership explored. It has been argued that models of care and support are increasingly complex and that within such a context previous leadership approaches may not be adequate. Relational and shared leadership has thus been proposed as a more fitting approach to meet current and future challenges.

Key Concepts Discussed

- **Models of care** – the different ways in which services for people who experience intellectual disabilities have been structured, organised and promoted through policy and legislation. These have varied over time and also between countries.
- **Values** – these are the principles that underpin models of care and reflect how society views people who experience intellectual disabilities. Views regarding the nature of intellectual disabilities have also varied over time and continue to vary between countries.
- **Leadership capacity** – within the context of this chapter, this has two dimensions. First, the overall capacity and capability within organisations to ensure effective leadership. Second, the ability of individuals at all levels within services to develop and use effective leadership skills.
- **The context of leadership** – this relates to the environment within which leadership occurs and is shaped by a range of factors including models of care, the underpinning

value base, policies, economic constraints and the needs of people who experience intellectual disabilities.

Key Readings

■ Buchner, T. (2009). Deinstitutionalisation and community living for people with intellectual disabilities in Austria: History, policies, implementation and research. *Tizard Learning Disability Review 14*(1), 4–13.
■ Menon, D.K., Kishore, M.T., Sivakumer, T. et al. (2017). The national trust: A viable model of care for adults with intellectual disabilities in India. *Journal of Intellectual Disabilities 21*(3), 259–269.

Examples of Studies

■ Bigby, C. and Beadle-Brown, J. (2018). Improving quality of life outcomes in supported accommodation for people with intellectual disability: What makes a difference (Review article). *Journal of Applied Research in Intellectual Disabilities 31*(2), 2182–2200.
■ Buntix, W.H.E. and Schalock, R.L. (2010). Models of disability, quality of life and individualised supports: Implications for professional practice in intellectual disability. *Journal of Policy and Practice in Intellectual Disability 7*(4), 283–294.

Useful Websites

■ Intellectual Disability and Health – Changing Values http://www.intellectualdisability.info/changing-values
■ Open University Social History of Learning Disabilities Website http://www.open.ac.uk/health-and-social-care/research/shld/

References

Áras Attracta Swinford Review Group (2016). *Key Messages*. Dublin: Áras Attracta Swinford Review Group.

Bank-Mikkelson, N. (1980). Denmark. In: R.J. Flynn and K.E. Nitsch (Eds.) *Normalisation, Social Integration and Community Services*. Austin, TX: Pro-Ed. pp. 51–70.

BBC (2011). *Undercover Care: The Abuse Uncovered*. London: BBC Panorama. BBC One. 31 May 2011.

Blatt, B. and Kaplan, F. (1966). *Christmas in Purgatory. A Photographic Essay on Mental Retardation*. (2nd edition) Boston, MA: Allyn and Bacon.

Brown, H. and Smith, H. (Eds.) (1992). *Normalisation: A Reader for the Nineties*. London: Routledge.

Caldwell, J. (2010). Leadership development of individuals with developmental disabilities in the self-advocacy movement. *Journal of Intellectual Disability Research 54*(11), 1004–1014.

Chappell, A.L. (1997). From normalisation to where? In: L. Barton and M. Oliver (Eds.) *Disability Studies: Past, Present and Future*. Leeds: The Disability Press. pp. 45–62. Online: Available at: https://disability-studies.leeds.ac.uk/wp-content/uploads/sites/40/library/Chappell-chapter3.pdf. Accessed 8 July 2018.

Clarke, N. (2018). *Relational Leadership: Theory, Practice and Development*. Abingdon: Routledge.

Crow, L. (1996). Including all our lives: Renewing the social model of disability. In: J. Morris (Ed.) *Encounters with Strangers. Feminism and Disability 7*. London: The Women's Press. pp. 206–226.

Cummins, R. (2016). At society's pleasure: The rise and fall of services to people with an intellectual disability. In: R. Jackson and M. Lyons (Eds.) *Community Care and Inclusion*. Edinburgh: Floris Books. pp. 42–56.

Emerson, E. (1992). What is normalisation? In: H. Brown and H. Smith (Eds.) *Normalisation: A Reader for the Nineties*. London: Routledge. pp. 1–18.

Ferguson, D.L., Ferguson, P.M. and Wehmeyer, M.L. (2013). The self-advocacy movement. Late modern times (1980CE to present). In: M.L. Wehmeyer (Ed.) *The Story of Intellectual Disability. An Evolution of Meaning, Understanding and Public Perception*. Baltimore, MD: Paul Brookes Publishing. pp. 233–277.

Flynn, M. (2012). *Winterbourne View. A Serious Case Review.* Gloucs: South Gloucestershire Safeguarding Adults Board.

Howe, G., Adams, H.L., Cole, J., Davis, D.R. and Jenkins, G.E. (1969). *The Ely Inquiry.* Online: Available at: https://www.soc health.co.uk/national-health-service/democracy-involvement-a nd-accountability-in-health/complaints-regulation-and-enquri es/report-of-the-committee-of-inquiry-into-allegations-of-ill-tre atment-of-patients-and-other-irregularities-at-the-ely-hospital-c ardiff-1969/. Accessed 2 June 2018.

Inclusion International (2016). *Self-Advocacy for Inclusion: A Global Report.* London: Inclusion International.

Jackson, R. (2011). Challenges of residential and community care: 'The times they are a-changing'. *Journal of Intellectual Disability Research 55*(9), 933–944.

Jackson, R. (2016). Introduction. In: R. Jackson and M. Lyons. (Eds.) *Community Care and Inclusion.* Edinburgh: Floris Books. pp. 15–27.

Nirje, B. (1969). The normalization principle and its human management implications. In: R.N. Kugel and W. Wolfensberger (Eds.) *Changing Patterns in Residential Services for the Mentally Retarded.* Washington DC: Presidential Committee on Mental Retardation.

Northway, R. (2018a). Knowledge, time and change. *Journal of Intellectual Disabilities 22*(2), 111–112.

Northway, R. (2018b). The need to move 'upstream'. *Journal of Intellectual Disabilities 22*(3), 211–212.

Oliver, M. (1996). *Understanding Disability. From Theory to Practice.* Basingstoke: Macmillan.

Pring, J. (2011). *Longcare Survivors. The Biography of a Care Scandal.* York: Disability News Service.

RTE Investigations Unit (2014). *Inside Bungalow 3.* Dublin: RTE Prime Time Investigates. Online: Available at: https://www.rte.ie/news/player/prime-time-web/2014/1209/. Accessed 18 April 2018.

Ryan, J. and Thomas, F. (1987). *The Politics of Mental Handicap.* (2nd edition) London: Free Association Books.

UN General Assembly (1948). Universal Declaration of Human Rights, Online: Available at: http://www.un.org/en/universal -declaration-human-rights/. Accessed 30 January 2019.

United Nations (2006). *Convention on the Rights of Persons with Disabilities.* Geneva: United Nations.

Weberg, D. (2012). Complexity leadership: A healthcare imperative. *Nursing Forum 47*(4), 268–277.

Wehmeyer, M.L. and Schalock, R.L. (2013). The parent movement. Late modern times. In: M.L. Wehmeyer (Ed.) *The Story of Intellectual Disability. An Evolution of Meaning, Understanding and Public Perception.* Baltimore: Paul Brookes Publishing. pp. 187–231.

Welsh Office (1983). *The All Wales Strategy for the Development of Services for Mentally Handicapped People.* Cardiff: Welsh Office.

Williams, P. and Tyne, A. (1988). Exploring values as the basis for service development. In: D. Towell (Ed.) *An Ordinary Life in Practice.* London: King Edward's Hospital Fund for London. pp. 23–31.

Wolfensberger, W. (1972). *The Principle of Normalization in Human Services.* Toronto: National Institute on Mental Retardation.

Wolfensberger, W. (1992). *A Brief Introduction to Social Role Valorization as a High-Order Concept for Structuring Human Services.* (2nd edition) Syracuse, NY: Training Institute for Human Service Planning, Leadership and Change Agentry.

LEADERSHIP FOR IMPROVING AND ENERGISING

II

LEADERSHIP FOR IMPROVING AND ENERGISING

Chapter 3

Distributed Leadership – An Alternative Approach for Intellectual Disability?

Elizabeth A. Curtis

Contents

Chapter Topics

- **Significance of leadership in health and social care**
- **An alternative approach to leadership: less leaderism and more participation**
- **Genesis of distributed leadership (DL)**
- **Leadership for contemporary nursing and healthcare**
- **A tentative guide for initiating DL in nursing practice**

Introduction

Leadership has generated interest among people for a long time and much has been written about it too. This interest and fascination with the topic may in part be due to its enigmatic nature and partly because at some point of our lives most of us will be affected by it (Yukl, 1998, 2013). Furthermore, the topic of leadership and its research is of concern because it can inform us not only about who we are as individuals but also about who we are as members of a group and wider society (Curtis and Cullen, 2017). To stress the importance of leadership further, Hughes et al. (2006: 19) remind us in the first chapter of their book *Leadership: Enhancing the Lessons of Experience* that "leadership is everyone's business and everyone's responsibility". Leadership however, is not always an easy process and this was eloquently expressed by Warren Bennis when writing about the challenges of leadership. He stated "In the best of times, we tend to forget how urgent the study of leadership is. But leadership always matters, and it has never mattered more than it does now" (Bennis, 2007: 2). Leadership is also critical when teams or organisational systems are undergoing change. This is especially relevant within the context of nursing and intellectual disability services given that in recent years several deficiencies in care have been reported both nationally and internationally (Northway, 2017; Áras Attracta Swinford Review Group, 2016).

This chapter suggests DL as an alternative approach to leadership and puts forward a tentative guide for supporting organisational change and development within intellectual disability services. The chapter does not offer a comprehensive account of DL. Rather, its intention is to introduce nurses and other care staff to the concept and draw attention to key considerations that might be useful for creating an environment where DL could be used as a driver for supporting care and changes in intellectual disability. The chapter begins by reminding the reader about the importance of leadership in health and social care and then explains how DL has been conceptualised and defined in the literature. Next, it summarises the theoretical and historical roots of the concept. A synopsis of the empirical evidence on DL is provided and its relevance and application within healthcare discussed. The chapter concludes by putting forward a tentative guide for introducing DL in intellectual disability services.

Importance of Leadership in Health and Social Care

Effective leadership is central to promoting the quality and integration of healthcare (Sfantou et al., 2017), improving performance and organisational citizenship behaviour (Kacmar et al., 2012; Braun et al., 2013), quality care (Gille et al., 2015), and organisational commitment (Paliszkiewicz et al., 2014).

In the last two decades, healthcare organisations and care facilities have been scrutinised intensely due to inadequate standards of care and poor performance (Curtis and Cullen, 2017). Examples include the Winterbourne View scandal in South Gloucestershire, England (Bubb, 2014), the Áras Attracta care home in Mayo, Ireland (Áras Attracta Swinford Review Group, 2016), and the maternal death of Savita Halappanavar in Ireland (HSE, 2013). The Winterbourne View Report cited a "lack of local leadership and weak accountability" (Bubb, 2014: 25) and the Áras Attracta Report contained a section entitled "Strengthening and Enhancing the Leadership and Management" with a key recommendation to implement a leadership development programme (Áras Attracta Swinford Review Group, 2016: 13). What these reports seem to suggest is that inappropriate or inadequate leadership is associated with poor patient/client care outcomes and as indicated above most have called for improved leadership and leadership development programmes. A reasonable question to ask at this juncture is what evidence exists to support the claim that leadership can indeed improve many variables including patient/client care outcomes?

Writing in the editorial of *Journal of Nursing Management* Wong (2015) suggested that while a large body of research demonstrates associations between leadership and better patient/client care outcomes (e.g., lower medication errors) future research needs to include longitudinal designs and ascertain causal connections among variables. Examples of studies showing a connection between leadership and patient/client care outcomes include a study by Cummings et al. (2010), who found that nursing leadership did in fact have an impact on patient mortality – staff who practised resonant (emotionally intelligent) leadership could result in lower 30-day mortality. A systematic review carried out by Wong et al. (2013) reported a definite link between supportive leadership and patient outcomes such as lower medication errors, patient mortality, hospital-acquired infections and higher patient satisfaction (Wong, 2015). These associations according to Wong et al. (2013) may be due to the fact that supportive leadership may result in better work environments (good staffing levels, improved resources, and care practices) which may in turn help reduce mortality. Agnew and Flin (2014) carried out a study to investigate the leadership behaviours practised by senior charge nurses and determine their association with safety outcomes. The findings indicated that relations-oriented and task-oriented behaviours were generally used but that during challenging situations task-oriented behaviours predominated. Interestingly, nurses' ratings of their senior charge nurses' leadership behaviours (monitoring and recognising) were associated with staff compliance while the senior charge nurses' self-ratings demonstrated that supportive behaviours were associated with lower infection rates. In a similar vein, Paquet et al. (2013: 87) explored the role of thirteen work environment (psychosocial) variables as predictors of patient outcomes. The results suggest that four perceptions of work environment ("apparent social support from supervisor, appreciation of workload demands, pride in being part of one's work team, and effort/reward balance") were linked to reduced medication errors and reduced length of stay in care units.

In addition to associations between leadership and patient care outcomes other research studies have demonstrated relationships between leadership and improved performance (Wong and Cummings, 2009; Paliszkiewicz et al., 2014; Brown et al., 2015). Such findings are no doubt significant given that most organisations strive to increase performance and address financial pressures but a word of caution here: due consideration must be given to the unintentional consequences (e.g., breakdown in standards of care) that could occur when applying systems and activities designed to increase efficiency of services (Cohn, 2015). Additional variables that have been examined for associations with leadership include job satisfaction and work environments. A Canadian study (Hayward et al., 2016) found that nurses left their jobs because of inadequate leadership, poor professional relationships with physicians and negative work environments. Similarly, Galleta et al. (2013) reported that intention to leave a job was drastically reduced when relationships between nurses and leaders were good.

While it is well recognised that most health professionals receive lectures in leadership at some stage during their respective undergraduate programmes of study (Ahmed et al., 2015; Ailey et al., 2015) and that several universities offer leadership programmes at postgraduate level, it is important to point out that the content of these programmes can vary and may not suit the needs of everyone (Curtis et al., 2011). Moreover, leadership programmes in health have been criticised because they do not for example (a) include continuing learning opportunities that take into account participants' experiences from practice and (b) continue to portray leadership from an individual/ leader-centric perspective (Fulop and Day, 2010). Recently, there has been a call for a different kind of leadership in healthcare: one that is patient/client focused and addresses care in an integrated way. This, according to Ahmed et al. (2015) requires a change from the current situation where leadership is centred on one individual (concentrated or heroic leadership) to a more participative or distributed approach where all individuals can participate in leadership. The chapter now moves on to address this alternative approach – DL.

Why Distributed Leadership and What Is it?

For almost 60 years, research has focused on organisations with hierarchical structures and, whether intended or not, this has contributed to the view that leadership, knowledge, and decision-making are all reserved for those in charge (managerial or supervisory positions). Such a centralised view of leadership has resulted in key individuals, usually those in senior positions, being referred to as *leaders* for other employees, who are generally known as *followers*. Interestingly, the claim that centralised leadership (single leader) has a positive impact on performance lacks research evidence (Thorpe et al., 2007, as cited by Thorpe et al., 2011). We also know that change is inevitable for organisations and that the pace at which this is taking place is greater now than it has ever been. This means that organisations now have to respond speedily to issues and problems, including redesigning jobs and management approaches currently in use and improving motivation. Organisational structures including those in healthcare have also had to change in order to deal with the challenges that can arise from rapid change. Whatever the changes taking place in nursing and healthcare it is now evident that leadership must also change from a concentrated approach (single person) to a distributed or collective effort, where all employees can participate in decision-making and in developing the organisation's core vision (Ahmed et al., 2015; Harris, 2013; Thorpe et al., 2011). As already alluded to, there have been many failures in the quality of patient care and several unnecessary deaths in our health service facilities so the time is right for adopting a different kind of leadership approach. This is supported by the lack of research evidence to support the link between concentrated leadership and performance that is so often claimed and a call for researchers to move away from research agendas that support concentrated leadership (Thorpe et al., 2011).

So, what then is DL? According to Harris (2013) the term is used differently by different people; for example, the term is often used inappropriately to describe shared and collaborative leadership. This variation of usage not only leads to mixed-up meanings and interpretations but also potential difficulties when researching the concept. Furthermore, suggesting that DL is the converse of hierarchical leadership or a constituent part of a mixed or hybrid approach to leadership further complicates the meaning of the term. Harris (2013) further argues that DL is an alternative approach to leadership and not necessarily the reverse of traditional leadership or a component of a mixed or combined model. Bolden (2011: 251) suggests that DL has encouraged a move away "from the attributes and behaviours of individual leaders ... to a more systemic perspective, whereby leadership is conceived of as a collective social process emerging through the interactions of multiple actors". In her paper, Angelle (2010) made the point that to understand DL one must consider what the term is not. For example, DL is not about allocating tasks or activities and delegating responsibilities. In concluding this section attention is drawn to two major reviews of the literature on DL. The first, reported in 2003 concluded that there were few clear definitions of the concept and those that were explored were dissimilar (Bennett et al., 2003). The second, a meta-analysis reported in 2015 examined literature from 2002 to 2013 and the authors concluded "that over the past decade, research seems to have enriched the discussion of how to fill the gap of conceptualising DL, but has not yet reached a consensus on what DL is" (Tian et al., 2016: 152). Harris and DeFlaminis (2016: 142) disagreed with such comments and stated in their article "recently, an account of the literature on DL concluded, rather pessimistically, that the impact of DL remains questionable". Their justification for taking such a stance was based on the fact that relevant international literature was not included in the paper by Tian and colleagues. Additional information about DL will be addressed later in the chapter.

Theoretical Origins of Distributed Leadership

You would be forgiven for thinking that DL is a recent phenomenon given the huge interest in the topic and the increased volume of literature since the start of the millennium. In fact its origins are much older (Bolden, 2011). DL can be traced back to 1250 BC which suggests that it is probably one of the oldest leadership approaches used for achieving organisational goals (Oduro, 2004: 4). The theoretical genesis of the concept is however, much later: perhaps the early 1920s or sooner (Bolden, 2011). According to Gronn (2000) the idea of DL was first addressed by Gibb (1954) who claimed that leadership functions are best carried out by a group. In spite of its early origins the concept remained underdeveloped until the 1980s (Brown and Hosking, 1986) and 1990s (Leithwood et al., 1997). To gain a better understanding of the theoretical origins of the concept I would suggest you read Richard Bolden's paper (Bolden, 2011) as it provides names and references of some of the earliest researchers. For the purposes of this chapter the most contemporary standpoint will be summarised.

The person credited as the most contemporary theorist of distributed leadership is James P. Spillane (Spillane, 2006). His work was shaped by cognitive psychology, in particular distributed cognition and activity theory: both of which emphasise the importance of context and its effect on human interaction and learning. Distributed cognition infers that learning occurs via interactions within and between several teams. In health and social care this could be applied in the work of intellectual disability nurses through key worker groups, clinical nurse managers from different sub specialities and work improvement teams (Harris, 2008). This symbiosis between an individual and the context or environment suggests that human activity is distributed. Spillane developed the theory on three key assumptions: that leadership is about practice rather than leaders and their roles; that leadership practice is concerned with several leaders, followers, and the specific context; and that distributed leadership is not about the actions of people but rather the interactions among them (Spillane, 2005; Johnston, 2015).

Overview of Distributed Leadership

Distributed leadership promotes the view that people work in a way that combines the knowledge, abilities, and skills of several people to achieve goals rather than through the efforts of concentrated, heroic (single person) types of leadership where one individual runs the show. Distributed leadership accepts that expert knowledge can come from many people rather than a few; thus opening opportunities for leadership to develop or materialise from several people within a team or organisation. Some may argue that distributed leadership is about shared leadership but Spillane believes that distributed leadership goes beyond shared leadership: a leader and several other leaders and what Spillane referred to as the "leader-plus aspect" (Spillane, 2006: 3). Although Spillane considered the "leader-plus aspect" to be important he indicated that it is not adequate given that it does not take into account leadership practice. DL is concerned with the combined interactions among leaders, followers and the situation or context. According to Spillane "the situation of leadership isn't just the context within which leadership practice unfolds; it is a defining element of leadership practice" (Spillane, 2006: 4). He further explains that distributed leadership has three important components: leadership practice, interactions among leaders, followers and the situation, and the situation or context (tools and routines). Spillane sums up distributed leadership beautifully in the following passage:

> From a distributive perspective, leadership involves mortals as well as heroes. It involves the many and not just the few. It is about leadership practice, not simply roles and positions. And leadership practice is about interactions, not just the actions of heroes.
>
> **(Spillane, 2006: 4)**

Leadership Practice

As stated previously, distributed leadership goes beyond shared leadership; its emphasis is leadership practice. While there is a prolific amount of reported research on leadership many of the studies explore what leaders do (leadership research tends to focus on people, structures, roles, and routines) rather than the practice of leadership or how leadership is enacted (Johnston, 2015; Currie and Lockett, 2011; Spillane, 2006). Furthermore, accounts of successful effective leadership seem to be associated with a single leader or with those who are in leadership positions. This association according to Spillane (2005) is ineffective for the following reasons. First, leadership practice generally requires several leaders, some of whom may have no formal leadership title while others may do. As a consequence, it is necessary to stop viewing leadership as a heroic approach and instead distribute leadership functions to those who have the knowledge and skills required for improving the team or organisation. Second, leadership practice is not about what leaders do to followers. Rather, followers are an essential element of DL practice. Third, leadership practice is not about what individuals do but rather the interactions among all individuals (Spillane, 2005). In other words, leadership practice from a distributed perspective is about the interactions among leaders, followers, and the setting when carrying out specific procedures or tasks: some of which may include, responsibility for procedure, apparatus required, and the goals to be achieved by carrying out the procedure (Johnston, 2015).

Distributing Leadership – Who and How?

Leadership distribution is an important consideration when deciding *who* to distribute leadership responsibilities to, and according to Harris (2008) two provisos are necessary for successful leadership distribution. First, leadership must be distributed to individuals who are knowledgeable or to those able to acquire proficiency to enable them to perform leadership functions. Second, for DL to be successful it must be planned and managed judiciously. In DL the nature of the problem, activity or task influences how leadership is distributed and leadership practice develops from the interactions among leaders, follow-ers, and situation – e.g., tools and routines – (Spillane, 2006). Consequently, there is no set formula for determining to whom leadership responsibilities should be distributed or where it might take place. Distribution can consist of approximately three to seven individuals, including nurse clinicians, administrators, specialist consultants, and other stakeholder groups (people with intellectual disabilities and their families). Furthermore, sev-eral leaders can be responsible for various leadership routines or tasks but the numbers participating will depend on the types of routines/tasks and activities required (Spillane, 2005). What is important here is that distribution takes into account the talent and experience of individuals irrespective of their grade or posi-tion within the team or organisation.

Deciding *how* leadership is distributed and who is responsi-ble for doing so are other key factors to consider. Harris's (2008) view is that distributed leadership does not follow a specific model or pre-prescribed approach. Rather, it develops or comes into view from within teams or organisations so that problems and difficulties can be resolved. Three methods have been put forward for how leadership responsibilities can be distributed and include "(a) design, (b) by default, and (c) through crisis" (Spillane, 2006: 41–42). *Design* refers to individual or shared decisions by designated and non-designated leaders and may involve setting up committees and structures. This however, is not the only approach that can be used to distribute leadership. Leadership distribution can also occur *by default* where lead-ers (Director of Nursing) take on leadership duties. This form of distribution takes time as leaders get to know each other's strengths and weaknesses, build trust and develop working rela-tionships. Lastly, leadership distribution can occur *through crisis*. Such a situation may occur in nursing practice when faced with an unexpected challenge or incident and designated leaders have to work with others to resolve the incident or problem. These approaches do not preclude each other and can work in partnership (Spillane, 2006; Johnston, 2015).

Distributed Leadership in Nursing and Healthcare

Leadership has played a significant role among healthcare professionals, policy makers and academics for a number of years and this interest shows no sign of abating (Martin et al., 2015; Chreim and MacNaughton, 2016). This appeal extends across many countries including the United Kingdom, the United States of America and Canada and in the majority of instances leadership endeavours are associated with improving effectiveness in services and patient care outcomes. In addition to this, several national scandals have resulted in many prominent investigations and published reports. For example, the Mid-Staffordshire National Health Service (NHS) enquiry (Francis, 2013), the maternal death in 2012 of Savita Halappanavar in Galway, Ireland (HSE, 2013) have highlighted failures and deficiencies in standards of care and triggered questions about leadership in the NHS and elsewhere (Martin et al., 2015).

Recommendations from the Francis Report for example, emphasised the need for improving quality and promoting a culture of honesty and patient-centred care. Two additional reasons for the huge interest in leadership are (a) the belief that leadership can improve organisational deficiencies and (b) increasing awareness of the limitations of individual/positional (heroic) leadership approaches (including transformational leadership) and the need to distribute leadership to all staff at the forefront of patient/client care (Currie and Lockett, 2011). This need for an alternative approach to leadership is further supported by other published material including, a Department of Health White Paper for the NHS (Department of Health, 2010) which stressed the need to distribute leadership to clinicians at the forefront of care, another document entitled *An NHS Leadership Team for the Future* (Ahmed et al., 2015) also called for a model of distributed leadership, The King's Fund (2015) emphasised the importance of leadership development as opposed to leader development, and an

Irish document entitled *A Strategic Framework for Reform of the Health Service 2012–2015* (Department of Health, 2012) reported the need to foster leadership capacity at clinical level within contemporary healthcare.

It is clear from the content in the preceding paragraphs that the discourse surrounding leadership in healthcare has been relentless and the general consensus is that leadership needs to move beyond a leader-centric approach to a more distributed model. The NHS in the UK for example, has singled out DL as a key element of policy which resulted in several leadership initiatives including setting up the NHS Leadership Academy in England, Northern Ireland, Scotland and Wales (Martin et al., 2015). Given this backdrop, a reasonable question to ask is how effective has the application of DL been in healthcare? In answering the question the first point to stress is that few research studies on DL in healthcare were located during a literature search, but those that were found are summarised here. In a study to examine the application of DL in the NHS, Martin et al. (2015: 25) reported that individuals who participated in the study were "sceptical about it and there was little accepted evidence that it would bring about a better state of affairs". In another study (Fitzgerald et al., 2013) to explore patterns of change leadership and whether these patterns were associated with service improvements the researchers reported (a) that change leadership that is distributed widely is associated with positive service outcomes, (b) clinical/managerial hybrid models (staff combine a clinical role with managerial responsibilities) occurred across a range of professions (e.g., nursing, medicine, midwifery) and that when collaborations and interactions within teams are good this can have a positive impact on performance, (c) that effective working relationships between healthcare professionals and management personnel are fundamental to a distributed approach to change leadership and can create "the organisational capacity to deliver service improvement" (Fitzgerald et al., 2013: 237). In their research in Canada, Chreim and MacNaughton

(2016: 209) reported that although "overlapping of leadership roles and responsibilities" in distributed leadership can pose problems it has advantages too (e.g., offers corroboration for leadership functions), provided that the "chain of responsibility" for dealing with difficulties is understood by everyone. Interestingly, these researchers found that distributing leadership roles to several individuals did not bring about "comprehensive leadership practices" within the team.

In another study in the UK, researchers McKee et al. (2013: 14) explored the views of senior healthcare staff (e.g., professionals, managers and policy makers at strategic level) about quality and safety in the NHS and the type of leadership required for improvement. The study was part of a large mixed methods research project but for the section of the study reported here interviews were conducted with 107 individuals from England and Wales. The findings suggest that participants acknowledged the importance of leadership in providing "safe high quality care". Participants also referred to "traditional, hierarchical" positional forms of leadership as well as distributed leadership involving individuals with specific knowledge and skills across different levels in the organisation. While they acknowledged that distributed leadership is central to patient/ client safety and quality care they also warned that distributed leadership could result in "confusion about who was in charge". Furthermore, participants felt that traditional concentrated leadership was required to supplement distributed leadership in order to provide "support and expertise" (McKee et al., 2013: 11). In concluding their article, McKee et al. (2013: 17) reported that all staff have leadership roles and are responsible for patient safety and quality but stated that participants in their study felt that any new approaches to leadership must be considered alongside "old" leadership (concentrated/hierarchical) and stressed that DL on its own "could have adverse or even perverse unintended consequences". A different viewpoint however, has been put forward by Hartley and Allison (2000: 38) who said that modernising and development is, in most instances, taking place under uncertainty and difficulty and that leadership approaches can no longer be about "command and control from 'the top' of the organisation" and has called for leadership in the public sector to be revised to reflect this.

Günzel-Jensen et al. (2018: 111, 123) examined the influence of three leadership styles (transformational, transactional and empowering) in promoting DL in a large hospital in Denmark. The results indicated that the three leadership styles had a significant positive effect on perceived "agency" (individual's intention to influence leadership rather than just accepting a leadership task that was delegated from a positional leader) in DL but that an empowering leadership style was the most positive in supporting DL. These researchers further suggest that empowering leaders appear to be able to garner better employee participation and generate conditions that are more amenable to implementing DL than transformational and transactional leaders can. These findings are particularly relevant to health and social care settings given that empowering leaders offer staff independence and autonomy in executing their duties in settings considered to be hierarchical, complicated and predetermined. Another noteworthy finding reported by Günzel-Jensen et al. (2018) was the significant negative association between organisational efficacy and employee participation in DL – which implies that respondents who perceived greater organisational efficacy (collective participation) were less inclined to participate in DL practices. Using video recordings to explore leadership behaviours in an operating theatre Rydenfalt et al. (2015) identified 248 leadership behaviours which they subsequently reduced to nine. These researchers found that although surgeons participated in leadership frequently so too did nurse anaesthetists and scrub nurses, and while some leadership behaviours were associated with specific professions others were distributed across the entire team. Worthy of note however, is that leadership behaviours associated with patient safety seemed to be distributed in nature. The researchers thus concluded that their findings challenge assumptions that leadership in the operating theatre is based on traditional leader-centric approaches (most senior surgeon is responsible for leadership).

To summarise, it would probably be fair to say that only a handful of studies have examined DL from a healthcare perspective. Some of these studies have indicated the need for a more inclusive model of leadership – e.g., DL – in healthcare given the complex and ever-changing nature of the healthcare environment. Others have suggested that hierarchical leadership was necessary alongside distributed leadership to provide focus, reinforcement, and expertise. It is evident therefore, that further research on distributed leadership in healthcare and specifically in nursing is needed before any conclusive views about its utility in clinical practice can be drawn.

Distributed Leadership in Practice: Some Suggestions

According to Bolden (2011) DL can take place in many ways and cites examples from four authors. He points out that although these frameworks were grounded in research carried out in schools they might be useful in other settings too. For example, frameworks by Gronn (2002) and Spillane (2006) emphasise the interactions between leaders, other team members, and the setting as well as the numerous methods of working with others to achieve shared goals and outcomes (all of these are practices and processes that can be found in many organisations not just schools). In summary, Gronn's (2002: 430) framework outlines three key components: "spontaneous collaboration", "intuitive working relations", and "institutionalised practices". I have chosen Gronn's framework as a potential approach for introducing DL in intellectual disability practice. However, the literature informs us that before introducing DL certain prerequisites must be fulfilled. Using Gronn's framework for DL and key prerequisites a tentative guide is put forward in Table 3.1 to assist in enacting distributed leadership.

Table 3.1 A Tentative Guide for Enacting Distributed Leadership in Clinical Practice

Distributed Leadership (DL) Approaches (Gronn, 2002)	Descriptions/Explanations
	Tentative Guide for Enacting Distributed Leadership
"Spontaneous collaboration"	Spillane (2006) considers leadership to be distributed practice. This implies that the focus of leadership is the interactions among several leaders. It is not about what a single leader, manager or anyone else knows or does. Rather, it is concerned with concerted or contrived effort. One way in which this can be enacted in practice is to bring together groups of employees from different levels in the team or organisation, with different knowledge, skills, and strengths to carry out a specific activity or project. The group or team is dissolved at the end of the project (Bolden, 2011).
"Intuitive working relations"	Over time, intuition may result in two or more employees coming together to work jointly on specific initiatives. Leadership in this instance emerges from the working relationship and this is recognised by colleagues as well as the partners themselves (Gronn, 2002). This is not an untypical phenomenon in nursing and social care given the strong emphasis on team working. Babiker et al. (2014) for example suggest that teamwork is required for the effective and efficient delivery of healthcare as well as minimising adverse events.
"Institutionalised practices"	This refers to structures within teams or organisations. If dissatisfaction with current structures arises this may act as a catalyst to introduce new structural designs. For example, if a leader-centric approach is in place then committees and teams can be established to bring about greater collaboration among all staff (Gronn, 2002; Bolden, 2011).

(Continued)

Table 3.1 (Continued)   A Tentative Guide for Enacting Distributed Leadership in Clinical Practice

Prerequisites for Distributed Leadership	Descriptions/Explanations
	Tentative Guide for Enacting Distributed Leadership
Trust and accountability	There can be no doubt that trust is essential to nursing practice and that it is positively associated with several organisational variables. For example, trust is critical to developing leadership and organisational citizenship behaviour (helpful activities that employees perform without being asked) as well as client care outcomes (Curtis and Cullen, 2017). To develop an ethos of trust many things can be done. Trust must begin at the top of the organisation with senior staff and it must be portrayed not only by how we communicate but also how we act. This is a key point as staff perceptions are formed by what they hear and see. Showing kindness and consideration are ingredients for building trust, therefore managers must be kind to staff and vice versa: when kindness is demonstrated in a team or organisation it communicates a powerful message – that the well-being of staff is imperative. Accountability is a necessary element of nursing practice since it supports client and patient safety and nurses are aware of this. Furthermore, accountability within the profession takes many forms. Every nurse is accountable to themselves, their profession, to clients and their relatives, to colleagues and their employers. Therefore, accountability must feature during all aspects of nursing practice and client interactions. Accountability in nursing has been articulated in the document *Scope of Nursing and Midwifery Practice Framework* (Nursing and Midwifery Board of Ireland, 2015).

(Continued)

Table 3.1 (Continued)   A Tentative Guide for Enacting Distributed Leadership in Clinical Practice

Prerequisites for Distributed Leadership	Tentative Guide for Enacting Distributed Leadership
	Descriptions/Explanations
Communication	In nursing and healthcare, communication is necessary for all aspects of work including leadership, change, quality and safety, and client-based activities (Wang et al., 2018). Moreover, communication that is honest and clear is considered an antecedent of trust. Therefore, nurses and managers must make every effort to be clear and honest when communicating with all employees (Curtis and Seery, 2017). Lastly, the views and opinions of employees are indispensable for promoting effective communication (Constantin and Baias, 2015) in organisations and this must form the foundation of any communication strategy that is developed in nursing and healthcare or during change efforts.
Individually perceived autonomy	Individual perceptions of autonomy are central to distributed leadership (Unterrainer et al., 2017). As such, healthcare facilities must create work environments that enable all staff to participate in leadership activities, meetings and discussions that will allow them to share knowledge and debate ideas that could lead to innovative ventures. To achieve this it is important that managers or employers avoid work activities that are reduced to routine tasks and commit to improving communication processes (Curtis, 2010).

(Continued)

Table 3.1 (Continued) A Tentative Guide for Enacting Distributed Leadership in Clinical Practice

Prerequisites for Distributed Leadership	*Tentative Guide for Enacting Distributed Leadership*
	Descriptions/Explanations
Learning and development	Ongoing learning and development is critical to the success of any organisation and therefore must be included in strategic agendas in order to promote skill development, employee engagement and retention. Learning opportunities are necessary for attracting and retaining staff which is currently a huge problem in the nursing profession. (Coffey and Collins, 2017). Managers therefore, must facilitate the learning and development needs of all staff and recognise the ongoing nature of such learning. Healthcare is continuing to experience major changes and the nursing profession will need to participate in these reforms (Finkelman, 2012). To do so will require additional competencies, skills and knowledge which can be achieved through specialised continuing professional development programmes.
Promoting empowering structures and teams	Teamwork is central to the development of DL so all staff members will have to become good team players. To achieve this will require a collective stance and contemporary knowledge and skills (Yammarino et al., 2012). Preparation is necessary for everyone: existing leaders as well as emerging leaders – before distributed leadership can be implemented. A structure that enables all staff to become involved in several groups or teams is crucial. For example, all nurses could participate in at least one standing committee that focuses on a specific issue e.g., advocacy committee. Such participation can provide opportunities for problem solving and improved decision-making processes (Grenda and Hackmann, 2014).

(Continued)

Table 3.1 (Continued)   A Tentative Guide for Enacting Distributed Leadership in Clinical Practice

Prerequisites for Distributed Leadership	Descriptions/Explanations
	Tentative Guide for Enacting Distributed Leadership
Commitment from senior management	Fundamental to effective DL is having committed managers. DL requires a highly collaborative environment and as such managers must believe in the importance of DL and work with staff cooperatively to achieve its implementation (Grenda and Hackmann, 2014). Management personnel together with recognised leaders must be willing to share power and responsibility with everyone. This, together with bottom-up processes can lead to employee empowerment and is consistent with humanistic management practices (Dierksmeier, 2016). Employee empowerment can be viewed in two ways. One view sees empowerment as a top-down approach (managers communicate team or organisational goals to be achieved) while the second view utilises a bottom-up method that stresses trust, ownership, and encourages employees to ask questions. In addition to giving commitment and support managers must also be proactive: identifying deficiencies in care practices and finding ways to put them right (Kodama and Fukahori, 2017).

(Continued)

Table 3.1 (Continued)   A Tentative Guide for Enacting Distributed Leadership in Clinical Practice

Prerequisites for Distributed Leadership	Descriptions/Explanations
	Tentative Guide for Enacting Distributed Leadership
Leadership and management	Assumptions that managers are characteristically leaders or that only managers can lead are erroneous. This is particularly important for those who view leadership as leader-follower or superior-subordinate dyads. Given that leadership is about influence then it can be theoretically ascribed to any individual or team in spite of any management structures. "Managers are no different from those they manage" (Gronn, 2002: 442). To compound this problem the terms leadership and management are often used interchangeably in the literature on nursing and the topic of management is often given greater credence in clinical practice and education (Curtis, 2018). As a consequence, leadership as stated already, is misperceived as the responsibility of those in management positions. In relation to distributed leadership it is necessary that other staff members take on leadership roles and that managers accept this critical responsibility.

(Continued)

Table 3.1 (Continued) A Tentative Guide for Enacting Distributed Leadership in Clinical Practice

	Tentative Guide for Enacting Distributed Leadership
Prerequisites for Distributed Leadership	**Descriptions/Explanations**
Organisational or team democracy	Research has shown a strong positive association between organisational democracy and "perceived participation in organisational decision-making" (Unterrainer et al., 2011: 128). This suggests that democratic structures and practices may be necessary for employees to actually engage in participation. This study also found a significant relationship between organisational democracy and "ethical orientation". In democratically run enterprises "political efficacy" is experienced and this in turn can lead to organisational citizenship behaviours not only at work but also in wider society (Unterrainer et al., 2011: 129). There is a chance that DL can be misconstrued as the delegation of duties/tasks if responsibility, authority and ownership are not given to employees (Unterrainer et al., 2017). In view of all this, it is suggested that organisational democracy is essential for developing DL in clinical practice. Therefore, managers must take steps to promote it at all levels in organisations and care facilities.
DL has positive outcomes for employees	This is an important concluding point. Awareness of the benefits of DL could help staff develop positive attitudes and a willingness to become involved in its introduction in clinical practice. Research has shown that DL practices increases occupational self-efficacy which in turn has a positive impact on work performance, staff job satisfaction, and well-being (Unterrainer et al., 2017). Also, evidence suggests that DL enables service improvement (Fitzgerald et al., 2013). Organising workshops to disseminate knowledge and exchange ideas about DL would be a useful activity throughout all stages of preparation.

Conclusion

As noted in the introduction to the chapter, publications on leadership whether in the form of books, or scholarly papers are plentiful across several disciplines including nursing and healthcare. Less prolific however, are books or book chapters on DL in nursing. The intent of this chapter was to introduce nurses and other care staff to the concept of DL. In doing so a number of key issues were addressed. As a starting point the reader was reminded about the importance of leadership in nursing and healthcare given its centrality in promoting quality and reducing incidences of poor client and patient care. The chapter then put forward reasons why DL might be an alternative to the more traditional centralised approach to leadership and reported that the term lacked a clear definition. In spite of this lack of clarity it was made clear in the literature that DL is not about allocating tasks or delegating responsibilities. Rather, it is an interactive process involving several individuals in a given situation. A summary of the scholarly literature on DL and its use in nursing and healthcare were provided and the chapter concluded by pointing out that DL can take place in many ways but that key criteria need to be fulfilled before DL can be introduced in clinical practice.

Key Concepts Discussed

▪ Leadership has played a central role in nursing and social care for several years and continues to be influential in contemporary healthcare, where it is considered necessary for strengthening working relationships, communication, and client and patient care outcomes.
▪ In recent years, several high-profile failures in healthcare have emphasised the importance of leadership and have

called for improved leadership practices in hospitals and other care facilities.

■ Leadership, a well-researched topic has been conceptualised in several ways and there are numerous theories reported in the scholarly literature. For decades leadership in nursing as well as healthcare has focused on individualism, where senior personnel assume leadership responsibilities in organisations.

■ Several documents and scholarly papers have called for a different kind of leadership in health and social care (e.g., Ahmed N., Ahmed F., Anis H., Carr P., Gauher S. and Rahman F. 2015; Beirne M. 2017); one that promotes participation and considers the talent of all employees. DL is one such approach being considered.

■ DL views leadership as a collective process involving several individuals and therefore brings into question the leader–follower dichotomy of leadership that dominated for so many years in nursing and healthcare.

■ DL is a relatively new concept in nursing and healthcare and as a consequence there is not a vast body of literature available. In spite of this, nurses and other healthcare professionals not in senior positions or formal leadership roles are leading change and clinical initiatives in practice. Such evidence of DL should be nurtured and supported through continuing professional development and education programmes.

■ The chapter concludes with a tentative guide (Table 3.1) that nurses and other social care professionals might find useful for introducing DL in clinical practice. The guide is made up of two components. The first component outlines Gronn's (2002) framework for DL practice and emphasises three ways in which leadership can be distributed. The second component proposes key prerequisites derived from scholarly literature that must be in place before DL can be enacted.

Key Readings on Distributed Leadership

- Beirne, M. (2017). The Reforming Appeal of Distributed Leadership. *British Journal of Healthcare Management* *23*(6), 262–270.

  This paper reports on the significance of DL in healthcare. It singles out key factors that enable or constrain DL processes and presents the findings from a review of relevant literature. Main findings to emerge include (a) clinical staff without formal leadership titles are driving important change initiatives and improvements (b) although DL is evident, constraints are present. It is suggested that more attention should be given to educational and continuing professional development programmes as these could be used to assist "ordinary leaders" in clinical practice. The paper concludes with implications for practice and research.

- Bennett, N., Wise, C., Woods, P.A. and Harvey, J.A. (2003). *Distributed Leadership: A Review of Literature.* National College for Schools Leadership. Online: Available at: https://www.researchgate.net/publication/42793697_ Distributed_Leadership_A_Review_of_Literature. Accessed on 16 April 2018.

  This report offers a useful summary of literature, identifies implications for professional development and suggests that a research agenda be set up to examine how research in DL is developed and how to measure its effectiveness.

- Bolden, R. (2011). Distributed Leadership in Organisations: A Review of Theory and Research. *International Journal of Management Reviews* *13*(3), 251–269.

  This paper addresses themes such as the theoretical origins of DL, DL and other related concepts, patterns, and outcomes of DL.

- Currie, G. and Lockett, A. (2011). Distributing Leadership in Health and Social Care: Concertive, Conjoint or

Collective? *International Journal of Management Reviews 13*(3), 286–300.

This in a very interesting paper. It examines different conceptualisations of DL and addresses critical issues such as (a) whether the health and social care context supports DL and (b) if governments promote DL in the public sector.

■ Harris, A. (2013). Distributed Leadership: Friend or Foe? *Educational Management Administration and Leadership. 41*(5), 545–554.

This article states that DL is now a well-known concept that has been practised in many schools. The paper goes on to address definitions of DL, empirical evidence to support it, and the implications from the evidence for those in positional leadership roles.

■ Martin, G., Beech, N., MacIntosh, R. and Bushfield, S. (2015). Potential Challenges Facing Distributed Leadership in Health Care: Evidence from the UK National Health Service. *Sociology of Health and Illness 37*(1), 14–19.

This is one of the few papers on DL available in healthcare.

■ Spillane, J.P. (2006). *Distributed Leadership.* San Francisco, CA: John Wiley and Sons, Inc.

This book is a good resource for those interested in implementing DL. It is written by one of the key proponents of DL and is concerned with school leadership. Nevertheless, the principles can be applied to other professional groups including nursing. The book is composed of four key sections written in a non-complicated way which makes it an enjoyable read.

■ Tian, M., Risku, M. and Collin, K. (2016). A Meta-analysis of Distributed Leadership from 2002 to 2013: Theory Development, Empirical Evidence and Future Research Focus. *Educational Management Administration and Leadership 44*(1), 146–164.

This article provides a meta-analysis of research on distributed leadership. Its purpose was to determine whether the two gaps identified in earlier literature had been filled by recent research. The authors concluded that although new research has enriched the discussion surrounding distributed leadership the two major research gaps identified in a previous review have still not been addressed adequately.

Examples of Studies about Distributed Leadership in Healthcare

■ Boak, G. (2015). Distributed Leadership, Team Working and Service Improvement in Healthcare. *Leadership in Health Services 28*(4), 332–344.

The purpose of the study was to examine the introduction of DL and teamwork in a physiotherapy department in England. Findings indicated that DL and team working were essential for change and that this approach to working resulted in improvements in waiting times.

■ Chreim, S. and MacNaughton, K. (2016). Distributed Leadership in Health Care Teams: Constellation Role Distribution and Leadership Practices. *Health Care Management Review 41*(3), 200–212.

Using a qualitative design, the authors explored how role boundaries within leadership are interpreted and how leadership practices interrelate with team dynamics. The findings demonstrated that leadership "constellations" can result in leadership role overlaps and that these intersecting responsibilities can result in benefits and does not necessarily lead to uncertainty or ambiguity.

■ Chreim, S., Williams, B.E., Janz, L. and Dastmalchian, A. (2010). Change Agency in a Primary Health Care Context: The Case of Distributed Leadership. *Health Care Management Review 35*(2), 187–199.

This study set out to understand the subtleties of DL using a qualitative design. The findings demonstrated that distributed leadership was important for influencing difficult and complicated change.

■ Fitzgerald, L., Ferlie, E., McGivern, G. and Buchannan, D. (2013). Distributed Leadership Patterns and Service Improvement: Evidence and Argument from English Healthcare. *The Leadership Quarterly 24*(1), 227–239.

Using a multiple case study design this study explored leadership patterns in complex organisations and their impact on change. The findings indicated that DL is associated with improving service outcomes and that "good pre-existing relationships underpin the capacity of distributed leadership to implement service improvements." (Fitzgerald et al., 227).

■ Martin, G., Beech, N., MacIntosh, R. and Bushfield, S. (2015). Potential Challenges Facing Distributed Leadership in Health Care: Evidence from the UK National Health Service. *Sociology of Health and Illness 37*(1), 14–29.

This study examined the meaning of DL and its usefulness in the NHS using qualitative data from three healthcare organisations that had adopted DL. The key findings suggest that on several occasions the views of powerful policymakers were addressed while the views of staff in the clinical areas (e.g., nurses) were unlikely to be discussed. The researchers also reported a number of problems with DL.

■ McKee, L., Charles, K., Dixon-Woods, M., Willars, J. and Martin, G. (2013). New and Distributed Leadership in Quality and Safety in Health Care, or 'Old' and Hierarchical? An Interview Study with Strategic Stakeholders. *Journal of Health Services Research and Policy 18*(2), 11–19.

The purpose of this study was to investigate the views of strategic level stakeholders about leadership for improving quality and safety in the NHS in the UK. 107 stakeholders were interviewed. The results showed that leadership was important for safeguarding quality care, that participants distinguished between traditional leader-centric leadership (positional leadership) and DL. Furthermore, the researchers reported that while there was definitely a case for using DL given that all staff have a role to play in maintaining safe high-quality care, participants felt that DL could lead to confusion regarding who was in charge.

■ Rydenfalt, C., Johansson, G., Odenrick, P., Akerman, K. and Larsson, P.A. (2015). Distributed Leadership in the Operating Room: A Naturalistic Observation Study. *Cognition, Technology and Work 17*(4), 451–460.

This observational study was carried out in an operating unit in Sweden. Its aim was to investigate leadership behaviours in the operating theatre and clarify how leadership is distributed across different professions. The researchers reported 248 leadership behaviours but these were finally reduced to nine leadership behaviour groups. This analysis process indicated that while surgeons provided most of the leadership, nurse anaesthetists and scrub nurses also participated in leadership. In addition, leadership activities/behaviours that were associated with patient safety "appeared to be more distributed" (Rydenfalt et al. 451).

Websites

■ Distributed leadership sources: Amazon.com https://www.amazon.com/slp/distributed-leadership/2hvnssrboboa6qt
■ Distributed leadership in schools | Amazon Official www.amazon.com/books/education
■ European School Heads Association http://www.esha.org/
■ European Policy Network on School Leadership http://www.schoolleadership.eu/
■ Researching distributed leadership | ALTC: Distributed Leadership www.distributedleadership.com.au/node/106

References

Agnew, C. and Flin, R. (2014). Senior Charge Nurses' Leadership Behaviours in Relation to Hospital Ward Safety: A Mixed Method Study. *International Journal of Nursing Studies 51*(5), 768–780.

Ahmed, N., Ahmed, F., Anis, H., Carr, P., Gauher, S. and Rahman, F. (2015). *An NHS Leadership Team for the Future*. London: Reform Research Trust.

Ailey, S., Lamb, K., Friese, T. and Christopher, B.A. (2015). Educating Nursing Students in Clinical Leadership. *Nursing Management 21*(9), 23–28.

Angelle, P.S. (2010). An Organisational Perspective of Distributed Leadership: A Portrait of a Middle School. *Research in Middle Level Education 33*(5), 1–16. DOI: 10.1080/19404476.1010.11462068. ONLINE: Available at: https://www.tandfonline.com/doi/abs/10.1080/19404476.2010.11462068. Accessed 9 April 2018.

Áras Attracta Swinford Review Group (2016). *What Matters Most.* Report Commissioned by National Director, Social Care Division. Dublin: Áras Attracta Swinford Review Group. Online: Available at: https://www.hse.ie/eng/services/publications/disability/aasrgwhatmattersmost.pdf. Accessed 21 March 2018.

Babiker, A., El Husseini, M., Al Nemri A., Al Frayh, A., Al Juryyan, N., Faki, M.O., Assiri, A., Al Saadi, M., Shaikh, F. and Al Zamil, F. (2014). Health Care Professional Development: Working as a Team to Improve Patient Care. *Sudanese Journal of Paediatrics 14*(2), 9–16.

Beirne, M. (2017). The Reforming Appeal of Distributed Leadership. *British Journal of Healthcare Management 23*(6), 262–270.

Bennett, N., Wise, C., Woods, P. and Harvey, J.A. (2003). *Distributed Leadership.* Nottingham: National College of School of Leadership. Online: Available at: oro.open.ac.uk/8534/1/bennett-distributed-leadership-full.pdf. Accessed 9 April 2018.

Bennis, W. (2007). The Challenges of Leadership in the Modern World. *American Psychologist 62*(1), 2–5.

Boak, G. (2015). Distributed Leadership, Team Working and Service Improvement in healthcare. *Leadership in Health Services 28*(4), 332–344.

Bolden, R. (2011). Distributed Leadership in Organisations: A Review of Theory and Research. *International Journal of Management Reviews 13*(3), 251–269.

Braun, S., Peus, C., Weisweiler, S. and Frey, D. (2013). Transformational Leadership, Job Satisfaction and Team Performance: A Multilevel Mediation Model of Trust. *The Leadership Quarterly 24*(1), 270–283.

Brown, M.M. and Hosking, D.D. (1986). Distributed Leadership and Skilled Performance as Successful Organisation in Social Movements. *Human Relations 39*(1), 65–79.

Brown, S., Gray, D., McHardy, J. and Taylor, K. (2015). Employee Trust and Workplace Performance. *Journal of Economic Behaviour and Organisation 116*(August), 361–378.

Bubb, S. (2014). *Winterbourne View – Time for Change: Transforming the Commissioning of Services for People with Learning Disabilities and/or Autism.* A Report by the Transforming Care and Commissioning Steering Group. Online: Available at: https://www.acevo.org.uk/.../STRICTLY%20EMBARGOED%200001%2026%20Nov. Accessed 21 March 2018.

Chreim, S. and MacNaughton, K. (2016). Distributed Leadership in Health Care: Constellation Role Distribution and Leadership Practices. *Health Care Management Review 41*(3), 200–212.

Chreim, S., Williams, B.E., Janz, L. and Dastmalchian, A. (2010). Change Agency in a Primary Health Care Context: The Case of Distributed Leadership. *Health Care Management Review 35*(2), 187–199.

Coffey, D. and Collins, M. (2017). Learning Organisations and Leadership. In: E.A. Curtis and J.G. Cullen (Eds) *Leadership and Change for the Health Professional.* London: Open University Press/McGraw Hill Education. pp. 52–65.

Cohn, S. (2015). Trust my Doctor, Trust my Pancreas: Trust as an Emergent Quality of Social Practice. *Philosophy, Ethics and Humanities in Medicine 10*, 1–9. DOI: 10.1186/s1310-015-0029-6.

Constantin, E.C. and Baias, C.C. (2015). Employee Voice: Key Factor in Internal Communication. *Social and Behavioural Sciences 191*, 975–978.

Cummings, G.G., Midodzi, W.K., Wong, C.A. and Estabrooks, C.A. (2010). The Contribution of Hospital Nursing Leadership Styles to 30-Day Patient Mortality. *Nursing Research 59*(5), 331–339.

Currie, G. and Lockett, A. (2011). Distributing Leadership in Health and Social Care: Concertive, Conjoint or Collective? *International Journal of Management Reviews 13*(3), 286–300.

Curtis, E.A. (2010). Work Motivation. In: A.M. Brady (Ed) *Leadership and Management in the Irish Health Service.* Dublin: Gill and Macmillan Ltd.

Curtis, E.A. (2018). Leadership in Nursing and Midwifery. In E.A. Curtis, C. Griffiths, C. Comiskey, F. O'Rourke, E. Duffy and F. Sheerin (Eds) *Nursing and Midwifery Career Guide: A Guide for Newly Qualified Nurses and Midwives in the Republic of Ireland*. Dublin: School of Nursing and Midwifery, Trinity College Dublin. pp. 26–27.

Curtis, E.A. and Cullen, J.G. (2017). *Leadership and Change for the Health Professional*. London: Open University Press/McGraw-Hill Education.

Curtis, E.A. and Seery, A. (2017). Trust and Leadership. In: E.A. Curtis and J.G. Cullen (Eds) *Leadership and Change for the Health Professional*. London: Open University Press/McGraw-Hill Education. pp. 112–127.

Curtis, E.A., Sheerin, F.K. and de Vries, J. (2011). Developing Leadership in Nursing: The Impact of Education and Training. *British Journal of Nursing 20*(6), 344–352.

Department of Health (2010). *Equity and Excellence: Liberating the NHS*. London: Department of Health. Online: Available at: https://assets.publishing.service.gov.uk/government/uploads/.../dh_117794.pdf. Accessed 8 May 2018.

Department of Health (2012). *A Strategic Framework for Reform of the Health Service 2012–2015*. Dublin: Department of Health.

Dierksmeier, C. (2016). What Is Humanistic about Humanistic management? *Humanistic Management Journal 1*(1), 9–32.

Finkelman, A. (2012). *Leadership and Management for Nurses*. Boston, MA: Pearson Education.

Fitzgerald, L., Ferlie, E., McGivern, G. and Buchanan, D. (2013). Distributed Leadership Patterns and Service Improvement: Evidence and Argument from English Healthcare. *The Leadership Quarterly 24*(1), 227–239.

Francis, R. (2013). *Report of the Mid Staffordshire NHS Foundation Trust Public Enquiry*. London: The Stationery Office.

Fulop, L. and Day, G.E. (2010). From Leader to Leadership: Clinician Managers and Where to Next? *Australian Health Review 34*(3), 344–351.

Galleta, M., Portoghese, I., Battistelli, A. and Leiter M. (2013). The Roles of Unit Leadership and Nurse-Physician Collaboration on Nursing Turnover Intention. *Journal of Advanced Nursing 69*(8), 1771–1784.

Gibb, C.A. (1954). Leadership. In: G. Lindzey (Ed) *Handbook of Social Psychology*. Reading, MA: Addison-Wesley. Vol. 2, pp. 877–917.

Gille, F., Smith, S. and Mays, N. (2015). Why Public Trust in Health Care Systems Matters and Deserves Greater Research Attention. *Journal of Health Service Research Policy 20*(1), 62–64.

Grenda, J.P. and Hackmann, D.G. (2014). Advantages and Challenges of Distributed Leadership in Middle-Level Schools. *National Association of Secondary School Principals (NASSP) Bulletin 98*(1), 53–74.

Gronn, P. (2000). Distributed Properties: A New Architecture for Leadership. *Educational Management and Administration 28*(3), 317–338.

Gronn, P. (2002). Distributed Leadership as a Unit of Analysis. *Leadership Quarterly 13*(4), 423–451.

Günzel-Jensen, F., Jain, A.K. and Kjeldsen, A.M. (2018). Distributed Leadership in Health Care: The Role of Formal Leadership Styles and Organisational Efficacy. *Leadership 14*(1), 110–133.

Harris, A. (2008). Distributed Leadership: According to the Evidence. *Journal of Educational Administration 46*(2), 172–188.

Harris, A. (2013). Distributed Leadership: Friend or Foe. *Educational Management Administration and Leadership 41*(5), 545–554.

Harris, A. and DeFlaminis, J. (2016). Distributed Leadership in Practice: Evidence, Misconceptions and Possibilities. *Management in Education 30*(4), 141–146.

Hartley, J. and Allison, M. (2000). The Role of Leadership in the Modernisation and Improvement of Public Services. *Public Money and Management 20*(2), 35–40.

Hayward, D., Bungay, V., Wolff, A.C. and MacDonald, V. (2016). A Qualitative Study of Experienced Nurses' Voluntary Turnover: Learning from Their Perspectives. *Journal of Clinical Nursing 25*(9–10), 1336–1345.

Health Service Executive (2013). *Investigation of Incident 50278 from Time of Patient's Self-Referral to Hospital on 21st October to Patient's Death on the 28th October 2012*. Online: Available at: www.the journal.ie/Savita-death-report-hse-949822. Accessed 21 March 2018.

Hughes, R.L., Ginnett, R.C. and Curphy, G.J. (2006). *Leadership: Enhancing the Lessons of Experience*. Boston, MA: McGraw-Hill.

Johnston, M.P. (2015). Distributed Leadership Theory for Investigating Teacher Librarian Leadership. *Schools Libraries Worldwide 21*(2), 39–57.

Kacmar, K.M., Bachrach, D.G., Harris, K.J. and Noble, D. (2012). Exploring the Role of Supervisor Trust in the Associations between Multiple Sources of Relationship Conflict and Organisational Citizenship Behaviour. *The Leadership Quarterly* *23*(1), 43–54.

Kodama, Y. and Fukahori, H. (2017). Nursing Managers' Attributes to Promote Change in Their Wards: A Qualitative Study. *Nursing Open*. DOI: 10.1002/nop2.87. Online: Available at: https://www.ncbi.nlm.nih.gov/pmc/articles/PMC5653397/. Accessed 14 June 2017.

Leithwood, K., Steinbach, R. and Ryan, S. (1997). Leadership and Team Learning in Secondary Schools. *School Leadership and Management* *17*(3), 306–326.

Martin, G., Beech, N., MacIntosh, R. and Bushfield, S. (2015). Potential Challenges Facing Distributed Leadership in Health Care: Evidence from the UK National Health Service. *Sociology of Health and Illness* *37*(1), 14–19.

McKee, L., Charles, K., Dixon-Woods, M., Willars, J. and Martin, G. (2013). New and Distributed Leadership in Quality and Safety in Health Care, or 'Old' and Hierarchical? An Interview Study with Strategic Stakeholders. *Journal of Health Services Research and Policy* *18*(Suppl. 2), 11–19.

Northway, R. (2017). Leadership and Patient Care Outcomes. In: E.A. Curtis and J.G. Cullen (Eds) *Leadership and Change for the Health Professional*. London: Open University Press/McGraw-Hill Education.

Nursing and Midwifery Board of Ireland. (2015). *Scope of Nursing and Midwifery Practice Framework*. Dublin: Nursing and Midwifery Board of Ireland.

Oduro, G.K.T. (2004). Distributed Leadership in Schools: What English Headteachers Say about the Pull and Push Factors. Paper Presented at the *British Educational Research Association Annual Conference*, University of Manchester, 16–18 September 2004. Online: Available at: www.leeds.ac.uk/educol/docuuments/00003673.htm. Accessed 10 April 2018.

Paliszkiewicz, J., Koohang, A., Goluchowski, J. and Nord J.H. (2014). Management Trust, Organisational Trust, and Organisational Performance: Advancing and Measuring a Theoretical Model. *Management and Production Engineering Review* *5*(1), 32–41.

Paquet, M., Courcy, F., Lavoie-Tremblay, M., Gagnon, S. and Maillet, S. (2013). Psychosocial Work Environment and Prediction of

Quality of Care Indicators in One Canadian Health Centre. *Worldviews on Evidence-Based Nursing/Sigma Theta Tau International 10*(2), 82–94.

Rydenfalt, C., Johansson, G., Odenrick, P., Akerman, K. and Larsson, P.A. (2015). Distributed Leadership in the Operating Room: A Naturalistic Observation Study. *Cognition, Technology and Work 17*(3), 451–460.

Sfantou, D.F., Laliotis, A., Patelarou, A.E., Sifaki-Pistolla, D., Matalliotakis, M. and Patelarou, E. (2017). Importance of Leadership Style towards Quality of Care Measures in Healthcare Settings. *Healthcare 5*73, DOI: 10.3390/healthcare5040073.

Spillane, J.P. (2005). Distributed Leadership. *The Educational Forum 69*(2), 143–150.

Spillane, J.P. (2006). *Distributed Leadership*. (1st edition) San Francisco, CA: Jossey-Bass.

The King's Fund (2015). *Leadership and Leadership Development in Health Care: The Evidence Base*. London: Faculty of Medical Leadership and Management.

Thorpe, R., Gold, J. and Lawler, J. (2011). Locating Distributed Leadership. *International Journal of Management Reviews 13*(3), 239–250.

Tian, M., Risku, M. and Collin, K. (2016) A Meta-Analysis of Distributed Leadership from 2002–2013: Theory Development, Empirical Evidence and Future Research Focus. *Educational Management Administration and Leadership 44*(1), 146–164.

Unterrainer, C., Palgi, M., Weber, W.G., Iwanowa, A. and Oesterreich, R. (2011). Structurally Anchored Organisational Democracy: Does It Reach the Employee? *Journal of Personnel Psychology 10*(3), 118–132.

Unterrainer, C., Jeppesen, H.J. and Jonsson, T.F. (2017). Distributed Leadership Agency and Its Relationship to Individual Autonomy and Occupational Self-Efficacy: A Two Wave-Mediation Study in Denmark. *Humanistic Management Journal 2*(1), 57–81.

Wang, Y.Y., Wan, Q.Q., Lin, F., Zhau, W.J. and Shang, S.M. (2018). Interventions to Improve Communication between Nurses and Physicians in the Intensive Care Unit: An Integrative Literature Review. *International Journal of Nursing Studies 5*(1), 81–88.

Wong, C.A. (2015). Connecting Nursing Leadership and Patient Outcomes: State of the Science. *Journal of Nursing Management 23*(3), 275–278.

Wong, C.A. and Cummings, G.G. (2009). The Influence of Authentic Leadership Behaviours on Trust and Work Outcomes of Health Care Staff. *Journal of Leadership Studies 3*(2), 6–23.

Wong, C.A., Cummings, G.G. and Ducharme, L. (2013). The Relationship Between Nursing Leadership and Patient Outcomes: A Systematic Review Update. *Journal of Nursing Management 21*(5), 709–724.

Yammarino, F.J., Salas, E., Serban, A., Shirreffs, K. and Shuffler, M.L. (2012). Collective Leadership Approaches: Putting the "we" in Leadership Science and Practice. *Industrial and Organisational Psychology 5*(4), 382–402.

Yukl, G. (1998). *Leadership in Organisations*. (4th edition) Upper Saddle River, NJ: Prentice-Hall International.

Yukl, G. (2013). *Leadership in Organisations*. (8th edition) Harrow: Pearson Education Limited.

Chapter 4

The Role of Leadership and Motivation During Change

Patrick Ryan and Morgan Danaher*

Contents

* The authors wish to acknowledge the work of Naoimh Howe and Julie Lynch,
  Research Assistants at the Department of Psychology, University of Limerick,
  Ireland.

Chapter Topics

- **Exploring changes in the field of intellectual disability**
- **Reviewing current literature on leadership, motivation and change management**
- **Translating scientific progress in leadership and motivation into current intellectual disability service provision and delivery**
- **Creating and maintaining a motivating work environment**

Introduction

While significant contributions have been offered to our understanding of leadership over the years, a clear operational definition of the concept has yet to be arrived at (Beck and Cowan, 2014; Spillane, 2012). Despite this, most would agree that leadership entails certain key functions such as determining objectives for a group or organisation, organising work activities to accomplish those objectives, motivating followers to achieve the objectives and enlisting support and cooperation from people outside the group or organisation (Yukl, 2011). Such activities, along with the qualities of a creative visionary, have long been at the fulcrum of what it means to be a leader. More recently, however, reference to leadership has been arising specifically in the context of managing change. Rapid developments across the political, economic and technological landscapes are pressuring companies and services to adapt and respond to these changes accordingly in order to remain competitive, enhance employee and customer satisfaction and lead the organisation down a path of continual improvement and sustainability. Effective leadership is required to bring about such effective change.

In recent years, the field of intellectual disability has witnessed a subtle yet fundamental shift in identity, ethos and culture. First and foremost, due to medical and technological advances, children with complex needs are surviving to adulthood and older people who experience intellectual disability are achieving greater longevity (Coppus, 2013). Secondly, service providers are slowly moving beyond a custodial approach to care focused on treatment and cure, to a more holistic view of people who experience intellectual disability that focuses on their needs as well as their education and skills development (Doody et al., 2012). Moreover, in recent decades, social policy direction and service providers are moving from closed systems (that viewed disabilities as defects i.e., medical model) to socio-ecological systems of disability that are connected to the community (Schalock and Verdugo, 2013). The ensuing closure of long-stay institutions and the development of community services such as family support and supported accommodation, is having radical policy implementation implications. The most striking of these is the move from institutionalised, vocation-oriented service management to individualised services that emphasise meaningful social inclusion and belonging (Power, 2013). Services need to be equipped to respond to such changes, highlighting the critical need for effective leadership to adapt to this dynamic landscape. Historically, leadership tended to be predicated on top-down, autocratic and one-directional styles. Such approaches may have been suitable in times when the primary preoccupation was with employee control versus employee engagement and human capital exploitation versus human capital management. Although we have long departed from overly autocratic or authoritarian approaches to leadership, it must still be acknowledged that leadership, motivation and models of change that are favourable to short-term, private-sector, competitive employment contexts may not be appropriate for application in an intellectual disability setting.

This chapter follows with an exploration of the widespread changes that the field of intellectual disabilities is currently experiencing, primarily to offer context but also to encourage the reader to consider such issues throughout the remainder of the chapter, wherein prominent and contemporary thought on leadership and motivation are discussed in greater detail. Current research on leadership and motivation during change will be translated into a tangible approach that may be useful for application in contemporary intellectual disability service provision and delivery. The chapter will conclude with practical suggestions for the reader, to encourage those working within intellectual disability settings to create and maintain a motivated working environment through a period of transformation.

Change and the Evolving Landscape of Intellectual Disability

With the technological, medical, political, economic and social developments of the past century, the concept of change and managing it successfully has become a pivotal concern for companies and organisations globally. Organisations do not operate within a vacuum but within a dynamic and relatively unpredictable macro-environment ensuring that change is one of few constants. Few psychological and socio-environmental topics have received more literary attention than change. It poses as a substantial challenge for those in leadership roles to continually grapple with change in their respective organisational systems to sustain a level of effectiveness and sustainability, not to mention actual delivery of a service. According to Bridges and Mitchell (2000), the working environment tends to be in such a continuous state of flux that yesterday's assumptions and practices are therefore obsolete today. Contemporary authors such as Burnes (2009) argue that change is becoming more frequent, is typically of a greater magnitude and is much less predictable than ever before. The field of intellectual disability offers a prime example in this regard. Into the new millennium, the area has witnessed multifaceted change across service culture, work practices, staff roles, client demographics and service user roles. Such changes are worthy of deeper exploration to contextualise a discussion around the role of leadership and motivation during change in this area.

Service Delivery

Historically, the provision and delivery of care for people who experience disability was offered in the form of institutional care characterised by containment and separation from the public and community life in general (Atherton, 2012). Over the following decades, encouraged by the independent living movement in the United States, advocates for people who experience intellectual disability began to cultivate a tentative new vision of integrated, inclusive services in Ireland. This radical shift in thinking about service delivery resulted in a departure from provider-led programmes in segregated settings, with greater emphasis placed on individualised, user-led supports directed to community inclusion and active citizenship instead.

Medical versus Social Model of Disability

The deinstitutionalisation movement of the 1960s occurred alongside a shift in thinking about disability, from a heavy focus on a medical model of disability to a social model of disability. The latter views disability as an interaction between a person's health condition and the physical and social environment, whereas the former reduces disability to individual deficit. Take, for example, a man in a wheelchair who cannot attend a job interview on the first floor of a building because there is no elevator, only a flight of stairs. The medical model would suggest that this issue is because of the wheelchair, whereas the social model would view the stairs as the disabling barrier.

Client Demographic

Due to widespread medical and technological advances, individuals with disability are living longer and, as such, are experiencing a wider range of physical, psychological and social care complexities than before. Services that do not respond to this ageing demographic risk neglecting the changing needs of people who experience intellectual disabilities as they move through the life cycle.

Person-Centred Planning

Grounded in the social model of disability with its roots in the independent living movement, the adaption of service provision towards person-centred planning departs substantially from the sole management of the individual's disability. Instead, it promotes discovering how a person with intellectual disability wants to live their life, encouraging and supporting them to realise this, building on their competencies and making use of their unique abilities to make a valued contribution to their community. The framework of person-centred planning has challenged individuals and organisations to move away from segregated service practices that limit people's social roles and citizenship and has led to a fundamental shift in thinking about the appropriate nature of supports for people who experience intellectual disability.

The challenge of reconfiguring and modernising the approach to intellectual disability services may be impeded by the fact that some care providers believe that their existing model of service delivery (carefully established around current policy and finance frameworks) works, and thus have little, if any, incentive to introduce change. More often than not, "a choice is made not to jeopardise 'what is' for 'what could be', resulting in a compromise that minimises the reform and settles for improvements in the existing system" (Health Service Executive, 2012: 63). The scale of change required to successfully navigate the field of intellectual disability towards an embedded culture of person-centredness and social inclusion requires strong leadership and motivation.

A Review of the Literature on Leadership, Motivation and Change

Contemporary leadership theory distributes itself across time and task, site and situation and people, along with their respective bodies and other leadership-making materials such as technology (Connaughton and Daly, 2005; Gronn, 2000; Sinclair, 2005). In an era of instant, global media saturation, historical leadership practices based on a masculine "Great Man" image have been linked with a tirade of high-profile scandals centring on abuse of power, corruption and greed. In response, organisational leadership operating within the realms of modern legislation has embraced an appetite for more authentic leadership, which suggests that leaders who are more authentic draw on life experiences, psychological capacities (i.e., hope, optimism, resilience and self-efficacy), sound moral perspective and supportive organisational climate to produce greater self-awareness and self-regulated positive behaviours. This, in turn, fosters the leaders' and followers' authenticity and development, resulting in well-being and sustainable, consistent performance (Avolio and Gardner, 2005; Gardner et al., 2005). Some of the more prominent and contemporary streams of thought in the field of leadership and motivation are offered below. Following this, their relevance to the process of managing change will be explored and linked back to the specific context of intellectual disability.

Leader–Member Exchange

Leadership models such as the leader–member exchange (LMX) have developed into a significant area of scientific inquiry, receiving considerable empirical research attention in the organisational sciences (Dulebohn et al., 2012). Specifically, LMX theory states that leaders vary their interactions across followers and, in doing so, determine their relationships with followers (Wakabayashi et al., 2005). Moreover, the quality of the relationship predicts different outcomes (Gerstner and Day, 1997), such as satisfaction or turnover intentions (Van Dyne et al., 2007; Liao et al., 2010). Such a depiction of leadership is commensurate with an overall constructivist approach to embracing creativity, innovation, sustainability and a focus on creating symbiotic interpersonal relations (Gagliardi and Czarniawska, 2006; Adler, 2006). This recognition of the role of individual difference lends itself to a more humanistic leadership praxis. Mengel (2012), for example, has integrated the work of Viktor Frankl (1985) and Steven Reiss (2008) and created a leadership model grounded in existentialism and motivational analysis. It is designed to be useful in changing leader mindsets from the sole pursuit of wealth and power to more meaningful aspirations. Frankl's motivational theory provides an anthropological basis for the importance of values in leadership processes and the need to create meaningful work environments (Mengel, 2012).

Reiss Motivational Profile (RMP)

The RMP is a scientifically developed standardised psychological measure that helps people discover their values, goals and personality. Through the development of this measure, Reiss (2008) argues that the pleasure principle does not suffice to adequately describe human behaviour, and suggests that pleasure and happiness are rather by-products of experiencing life in general where "desire, purpose, and goals, are the main differences between life as a biological mass, and life as a human being" (Reiss, 2008: 132). By embracing these desires as motivators, Reiss argues that we experience a general feeling that life has purpose. In the context of leadership and motivation, understanding such desires for purposeful living, can assist leaders in creating an environment that reflects a healthy, dynamic and sustainable ecological workspace that allows for the actualisation of personally held desires for professional fulfilment. This generates the empowerment and interdependence of individuals, teams and consequently the organisation itself, in contrast to traditional autocratic leadership styles that promote dependence. Reiss views social and economic structures as more or less holistic organisations; systemic wholes with a dynamic and unique identity (Lück, 2011).

Engagement

According to Swensen and colleagues (2016), the key to realising success is to achieve a return from engaged people. Engagement can be described in terms of the degree to which individuals are psychologically invested in the mission of the organisation, resulting in increased discretionary effort towards the goals. Such organisational citizenship behaviour enhances productivity and helps institutions compete with what limited resources they have. In healthcare, organisational citizenship behaviour promotes patient satisfaction, greater coordination among employees, lower turnover along with organisational adaptability and profitability (Koys, 2001; Podsakoff and MacKenzie, 1994). Leaders have a direct impact on engagement (i.e., organisational citizenship behaviour) by inspiring commitment, providing recognition and offering growth and development opportunities. Colleagues want to be appreciated for their work, to belong to a high-performing team, receive fair compensation and experience a sense of purpose in their work. These intrinsic motivators can be delivered consistently with coordinated leadership and aligned organisational design (McAlearney, 2006).

Job Demands–Resources Model

Contemporary work-related motivational models such as the Job Demands–Resources (JD–R) framework are based on humanistic principles that acknowledge the individual's capacity for self-regulation and inherent drive to self-actualisation, and how these drives can be both facilitated and interrupted. Understanding both the facilitators and barriers that underpin satisfaction are now seen as being fundamental to the successful negotiation of positive change. The JD–R model proposes that high job demands lead to strain and health impairment and that high resources lead to increased motivation and higher productivity (Schaufeli and Taris, 2014). When job demands are high, additional effort must be exerted to achieve the work goals and to prevent decreasing performance and such discretionary effort is attributed to physical and psychological costs, such as fatigue and irritability. Withdrawal, reduced motivation and disengagement act as self-protective strategies that prevent further energy depletion (Xanthopoulou et al., 2009). Job resources are defined as "physical, social, or organisational aspects of the job that may do any of the following: (a) be functional in achieving work goals; (b) reduce job demands and the associated physiological and psychological costs; (c) stimulate personal growth and development" (Demerouti et al., 2014: 501). They can also include feedback, job control and social support. The inclusion of micro-processes (such as perceptions, discreet emotions and cognitions) and macro- processes (such as the social–relational context) dynamically affect follower and leader outcomes in terms of successful change management (Dinh and Lord, 2012; Trichas and Schyns, 2012; Chang et al., 2011; DeRue and Ashford, 2010).

Reflection on Action

Reflection on action is a significant component of contemporary change leadership. Action research (AR) based leadership models embrace continuous loops of action and reflection, and purport that the notion of measurement is fundamental to successful change leadership. In a change process based on AR, change is imagined, instigated, trialled and reflected upon. Demonstrating the efficacy of AR in terms of developing organisational leadership, Lines and colleagues (2015) successfully deployed AR to empirically measure the impact of individual change management factors on minimising resistance from organisational members during an implementation project. Carver and Klien (2013) used AR to upgrade a university-based leadership preparation programme. Using examples drawn from an AR project with candidates on a master's level principal preparation programme, they demonstrated how the collection and analysis of candidate's written reflections informed their work as university faculty and supported cycles of continuous programme improvement.

Participative Leadership

At its core, participative leadership is a leadership approach that invites input from staff and involves employees across different levels of decision-making. This style of leadership involves inspiring people and organisations to expand their thinking and foster synergy. It also involves providing the opportunity for support staff to be involved in the development and implementation of user-friendly individual service plans which are devolved from person-centred plans generated by service users. Successful participative leaders perform high-quality functions related to communicating a shared vision.

Practice Leadership

Initially identified as an important factor in determining the quality of support for people who experience intellectual disability, practice leadership involves regularly giving feedback and modelling aspirational behaviour and being present often enough and for long enough to see how staff are working (Bould et al., 2016). For practice leaders to be considered credible, they need to be seen by staff as "talking the talk and walking the walk". Mansell and Beadle-Brown (2012) described the model of leadership as involving skilled professional advice and assistance as well as administrative control, and an educational and developmental role beyond that of simple direction. Such front line leadership focuses attention on typical and routine daily experiences observed from the macro perspective of the organisation but understood from the micro experience of the individual client. Such leaders work to create a dialogue with staff and service users where the mutual exploration of the relationships between the powerless and the powerful represents a useful starting point (Kielhofner, 2005).

Bringing about permanent change and organisation transformation is a multistage process that involves a clear vision of the future, communication to enhance knowledge/understanding, employing constructive engagement that involves empowering others to implement the change, generating short-term wins to provide immediate feedback and reinforcement, and anchoring the new approaches in the organisation's culture (Schalock and Verdugo, 2012). This approach is both liberating in its potential for distribution of responsibility for how service providers deliver their mission and stimulating in that, while it requires significant personal investment of intense energy and commitment, the reward will be experienced by many and not claimed, owned or rewarded through the identity or position of one individual.

Translating Current Knowledge on Leadership and Motivation During Change into Intellectual Disability Service Provision and Delivery

Over recent decades, the field of intellectual disability has experienced an accelerated process of reconfiguration and modernisation across multiple facets of service provision and delivery, to embrace the principles of person-centredness, an ageing demographic and an orientation towards the social model of disability. This process has acted as a catalyst for significant change for many service providers, depending on the gap that existed between their current and desired offerings. Given the historical framework within which services in intellectual disability operated, the scale of the challenge involved in preparing staff for such innovation must not be underestimated. Changes to programme design and content, adjustment and greater flexibility of staff roles, development of new skill sets, reframing power structures, advocating for policy and structure change and moving to keyworker interdisciplinary teams are just some examples of a "change is constant" dynamic that has underpinned the work experience in the intellectual disability sector. The landscape of intellectual disability is not alone in this, however, with the general leadership paradigm largely shifting from individual to collective, from control to learning, from self to self-in-relation and from power *over* to power *with* (Fletcher, 2004). An understanding of such contemporary thinking on leadership and motivation is particularly useful to identify the most appropriate strategies for managing change in the field of intellectual disability. The practical application of contemporary leadership theory can be translated to the management of change in intellectual disability service provision and delivery under the following headings: collaboration and consultation with staff and service users; distribution of leadership roles; enhancing personal and professional development of staff; and promotion of organisational learning through feedback and evaluation.

Collaboration and Consultation with Staff and Service Users

Leadership strategies that are fundamental to successful change management involve strong communication strategies and early consultation with all parties involved. Early user involvement with the design and implementation of change processes can generate enthusiasm for change implementation (Stratman and Roth, 2002; Bartunek et al., 1996). Similarly, extensive top-down and cross-functional communication and the creation of available support teams, particularly for staff based out in the community, can mitigate the impact of resistance to change and enhance implementation success (Zafar and Naveed, 2014).

To explore this further, consider the theory of reasoned action. Closely aligned to the JD–R model outlined earlier, in terms of its contemporary motivation literature, the theory of reasoned action asserts that the most important determinant of behaviour is behavioural intention i.e., the intended outcome of exercising certain behaviour (Montaño and Kasprzyk, 2015). Direct determinants of an individual's behavioural intention are their attitude towards performing the behaviour and their subjective norm associated with the behaviour. An individual will more likely demonstrate a certain behaviour if they are comfortable in doing so and if they perceive that energy expended will result in a positive outcome. This logic appears self-explanatory but reiterates the importance of strong communication plans in gaining support for change initiatives. Therefore, collaboration with staff directly involved in service provision will help to elucidate clearly their perception of training needs, not just pertinent to themselves but necessary for the interrelated subsystems of the entire organisation. This facilitates a sense of being worthy of opinion and of being listened to, which encourages staff to actively participate in decisions related to the desired change and enhances engagement with the process. Perhaps even more critically, it models in a practical and authentic way, the values to which many service providers aspire to for individuals who experience a disability. In other words, such proactive leadership collaboration becomes a readily available, implicit teaching and learning mechanism that can assist in the translation of policy statements into tangible practice which directly impacts on the experience of the person who ultimately uses the service.

Distribution of Leadership Roles

As important as it is to develop individual leaders, it is even more important to develop the collective leadership of an organisation. This includes all leaders, formal and informal, at all levels so that organisational mission and direction are aligned and congruent. Such distribution dilutes the position of power away from a small nucleus in the overall service system while maintaining points of responsibility to ensure efficient delivery of service. This concept of participatory leadership has gained traction in the field of disability as an approach that assimilates not only the contributions of staff but also service users. Different and diverse groups are empowered and enabled to contribute freely to the effective functioning of the overall system. In the context of intellectual disability, service users have increasing autonomy and control over the nature of the services that they receive, as well as who, when and how the services are delivered.

This concept of self-direction, based on the value of enhancing agentic experience, is predicated on the idea that individuals with disabilities possess unique, individualised knowledge of their personal and unique needs that service providers can never truly acquire (Nadash and Crisp, 2005; Yamada, 2001). They also have the right to formulate and lead opinion on a package of services that best reflect their preferences, values, needs and context at that point in time (Nadash, 1998). In this way, self-leadership, self-regulation and self-direction honours and facilitates the inherent competency and capability of individuals with disabilities to monitor and direct the services upon which they rely or assists them to work towards that purposeful goal.

Enhancing Personal and Professional Development of Staff

As humans, we tend to be creatures of habit and comfort across our personal and professional lives. Rapid developments in technology and economic fluctuations can accelerate the process of change in organisations, which can be unsettling for employees. By planning programmes of support that will enhance employees' personal and professional capacities, it is possible to increase the rate of change of management success, encourage a sense of belonging and promote engagement.

Opportunities for professional development will be particularly pertinent to the successful negotiation of change. In the field of intellectual disability, the concept of person-centred planning has challenged staff to move away from segregated service practices that limit people's social roles and citizenship. To ensure that all staff have a clear understanding of (and commitment to) the principles and practices of a person-centred approach, comprehensive training in individu-alised approaches to choice-making and planning should be offered. A key element of this training and development will be familiarisation with the concept of person-centredness and what it means for day-to-day practice within the service. This should be part of the induction and development of all staff, not only those involved in facilitating person-centred planning. Creating an organisational culture that favours a person-centred approach will also involve proofing all poli-cies for person-centredness and making sure that people who experience intellectual disability served by the organisation have structures through which they can contribute to service policy and evaluation (Health Service Executive, 2012).

In a similar vein, individuals who experience intellectual disability are achieving greater life longevity. Organisations should consider training and development opportunities that focus on equipping staff with the skills and knowledge to work with and provide care for an ageing demographic of clients with intellectual disability. For example, there are con-siderable staff numbers that require training and awareness in the Health Service Executive's Policy on Elder Abuse (HSE, 2012). With the growing number of adults who experience intellectual disability reaching the age of 65 years (and bear-ing in mind that the onset of characteristics associated with the vulnerability of older people can occur in the intellectually disabled population at an earlier age), there is an urgent need to develop staff competencies in developmental considerations that impact on policy and practice.

Providing opportunities for personal development may be just as crucial to successfully negotiating organisational change as offering professional development. Change, even when well intentioned, is of necessity destabilising and there-fore stress-provoking for employees. This is particularly the case if the change is comprehensive and targets not just prac-tice, but ethos, values and culture. Destabilisation can result in the perception of skill reduction, confusion regarding professional identity and regression to lower level functioning as a way of trying to contain feelings of being overwhelmed and undervalued – the exact opposite of what is required to initiate and sustain change momentum. Resilience training and stress management programmes can promote engagement and buffer the effects of stress that change may impose. For example, McConachie et al. (2014) demonstrated the effectiveness of an acceptance- and mindfulness-based intervention to reduce distress for staff. Positive psychological capital or resilience has been identified as antecedents of well-being (Higgs and Dulewicz, 2014) and a mediator of the relationship between leadership and employee creative performance behaviours (Gupta and Singh, 2014). Resilient individuals are better equipped to deal with stressful events or conditions at work (Luthans et al., 2013). Leadership practices including explicit acknowledgement of what is being undertaken, what is expected, curiosity as to what may go wrong, openness to unexpected outcomes, as well as the desired outcome, will assist in cultivating an organisational environment that facilitates resilience-building. Studies show that resilient individuals with a high level of positive emotions and the ability to manage negative emotions can find meaning and overcome stressful situations (Tugade et al., 2004; Cooper et al., 2013). For instance, a high engagement culture may create a supportive environment for employees to build resilience and develop coping strategies (Bowles and Cooper, 2012; Truss et al., 2013). Proactive leaders make this an explicit aspect of foundational and preparation work prior to engaging in major change and reform.

Promotion of Organisational Learning through Feedback, Measurement and Evaluation

A plan for embedding reflective practice and feedback mechanisms at all stages of the change process is essential to ensure that the change effort is regularly reviewed, refined and if necessary, refocused. Schalock and Verdugo (2013) have argued that most disabilities organisations are data rich and information poor. It is imperative to move beyond simply holding vast quantities of data, towards analysing and more importantly translating data into organisational practice in a tangible, measurable and meaningful way. The development of standardised data gathering and data management systems for planning services, identifying needs and monitoring provision should readily translate into the improvement and sustenance of the quality of life for people who experience intellectual disability. Organisations that deal so comprehensively with the lives of people also need to ensure that the data that formulates feedback is not solely being generated by reductionist, rigid, tick-box outcomes (often presented as task or behaviour) that fail to capture the real and lived experience of service users. Qualitative and phenomenological data, which drills into the micro-transactions between the person and the service, will ultimately enrich feedback mechanisms to key leaders in order to influence policy and practice decisions.

Recommendations for Creating and Maintaining a Motivating Work Environment

Cultivating a healthy, motivating working ecology and environment for employees is fundamental to the successful negotiation of change. For staff employed in the field of intellectual disability (in which new models of service delivery are being established, among myriad other changes), the following recommendations may be utilised to enhance motivation.

■ *Authentic, observable and proactive leadership.* Leaders at all levels need to be comfortable and adaptable in how they bring to action their leadership style, their leadership ethos and their leadership vision. Initiating and maintaining strong working relationships with all stakeholders lays the foundation for the efficient and effective management of change. While this is labour intensive initially, the basis for open, honest and reciprocal learning oriented communication will help to contain the natural apprehension that comes with any change initiative.

■ *Provide ongoing professional learning and development.* Offering employees the opportunity to stretch and enhance their professional competencies and ensuring they have the resources they need to carry out their work effectively will contribute to their sense of increased resourcefulness and act as a buffer against the demands of their roles. As an example, in the field of intellectual disability, training and development opportunities must focus on equipping staff with the skills and knowledge to work with and provide care for an ageing demographic of clients with intellectual disability.

■ *Cultivate personal growth and resilience.* Given that staff working with individuals who experience intellectual disability and challenging behaviour experience high levels of burnout and work-related stress, increased emphasis should be placed on offering interventions that cultivate resilience and coping strategies. This is of particular relevance at a time when the field of intellectual disability is experiencing substantial shifts in focus. Acceptance-based, mindfulness-based and stress management programmes offer a useful starting point in reducing distress amongst staff and emphasising the importance of a healthy work-life balance. Enhancing employee well-being may contribute to increased engagement. This, in turn, will have a positive influence on staff motivation.

■ *Promote empowerment, autonomy and job control.* Change management initiatives should entail involving the staff concerned and encouraging early participation in decisions prior to any implementation of change. In the case of a redirected focus on community-based care versus day-care, offering staff the opportunity to voice their opinion on this approach and aid in identifying the facilitators and barriers of negotiating this change within the context of intellectual disability delivery of service, generates enthusiasm and motivation for change implementation.

Conclusion

The demands placed on this new wave of professionals in the post-deinstitutionalisation, post-congregated settings era of intellectual disability service provision are undoubtedly more complex to understand, influence and control. Authoritarian power can no longer be relied upon to motivate and control staff or services users into preordained pathways of experience. The shifting landscape of intellectual disability service delivery requires a novel approach to leadership and motivation, one which departs substantially from traditional models based on rigid hierarchies and the power base of a small cohort of individuals. Throughout the chapter, the reader is encouraged to contemplate the utility of more contemporary styles of leadership and motivation for managing change, using well-established principles such as creating a shared vision, engaging key stakeholders (including service users) and adopting a comprehensive communications strategy. Inclusive and participative styles of leadership are likely to be most fruitful in eliciting successful change across the facets of intellectual disability service provision and delivery. Motivation for change and improvement in service provision become the natural outcome when the processes that underpin them and the people who are central to them are valued, understood, nurtured, and intrinsically and extrinsically rewarded. Effective leaders sustain, maintain and nurture these processes and are ultimately a primary source of motivation for all stakeholders in the complex ecology of service use and service provision.

Key Concepts Discussed

- Consideration of the changes that have taken place in the field of intellectual disability.
- Knowledge status in respect to leadership, motivation and change management.
- How scientific progress in leadership and motivation might be translated into current intellectual disability service provision and delivery.
- The creation and maintenance of a motivating work environment.

Key Readings on Motivation and Change

- Avolio, B.J., Walumbwa, F.O. and Weber, T.J., (2009). Leadership: Current theories, research, and future directions *Annual Review of Psychology 60*, 421–449.
- Beadle-Brown, J., Bigby, C. and Bould, E. (2015). Observing practice leadership in intellectual and developmental disability services. *Journal of Intellectual Disability Research 59*(12), 1081–1093.
- Beadle-Brown, J., Mansell, J., Ashman, B., Ockenden, J., Iles, R. and Whelton, B. (2014). Practice leadership and active support in residential services for people who experience intellectual disabilities: An exploratory study. *Journal of Intellectual Disability Research 58*, 838–850.
- Kotter, J. (2012). *Leading Change.* Boston, MA: Harvard Business Review Press.
- McCarron, M., Sheerin, F., Roche, L.., Ryan, A.M., Griffiths, C., Keenan, P., Doody, O., D'Eath, M., Burke, E. and McCallion, P. (2018). *Shaping the Future of Intellectual Disability Nursing in Ireland.* Dublin, Ireland: Health Services Executive.
- *New Directions – Review of HSE Day Services and Implementation Plan 2012–2016.* Dublin, Ireland: Health Service Executive.

References

Adler, N.J. (2006). The arts and leadership: Now that we can do anything; what will we do? *Academy of Management Learning and Education* 5(4), 486–499.

Atherton, H. (2012). Eugenics: The creation and maintenance of difference In: H. Atherton and D. Crickmore (Eds.) *Learning Disabilities: Towards Inclusion.* London: Churchill-Livingstone. pp. 35–52.

Avolio, B.J. and Gardner, W.L. (2005). Authentic leadership development: Getting to the root of positive forms of leadership. *The Leadership Quarterly* 16(3), 315–338.

Bartunek, J.M., Rouseeau, D.M., Rudoph, J.W. and DePalma, J.A. (1996). Participation, complexity, of understanding, and the assessment of organisational chang. *Academy of Management Proceedings* 42(2), 182–206.

Beck, D.E. and Cowan, C.C. (2014). *Spiral Dynamics: Mastering Values, Leadership and Change.* London: John Wiley and Sons.

Bould, E., Beadle-Brown, J., Bigby, C. and Iacono, T. (2016). The role of practice leadership in active support: Impact of practice leaders' presence in supported accommodation services. *International Journal of Developmental Disabilities* 64(2), 75–80.

Bowles, D. and Cooper, C.L. (2012). *The High Engagement Work Culture: Balancing Me and We.* London: Palgrave Macmillan.

Bridges, W. and Mitchell, S. (2000). Leading transition: A new model for change. *Leader to Leader* 16(Spring), 2694.

Burnes, B. (2009). Reflections: Ethics and organizational change – time for a return to lewinian values. *Journal of Change Management* 9(4), 359–381.

Carver, C.L. and Klein, C.S. (2013). Action research: A tool for promoting faculty development and continuous improvement in leadership preparation. *International Journal of Educational Leadership Preparation* 8(2), 162–177.

Chang, J.W., Sy, T. and Choi, J.N. (2011). Team emotional intelligence and performance: Interactive dynamics between leaders and members. *Small Group Research Journal* 43, 75–104.

Connaughton, S.L. and Daly, J.A. (2005). Leadership in the new millennium: Communicating beyond temporal, spatial, and geographical boundaries. *Annals of the International Communication Association* 29(1), 187–213.

Cooper, C.L., Flint-Taylor, J. and Pearn, M. (2013). *Building Resilience for Success: A Resource for Managers and Organisations*. London: Palgrave Macmillan.

Coppus, A.M. (2013). People with intellectual disability: What do we know about adulthood and life expectancy? *Developmental Disabilities Research Reviews 18*(1), 6–16. DOI: 10.1002/ddrr.1123.

Demerouti, E., Bakker, A.B. and Leiter, M. (2014). Burnout and job performance: The moderating role of selection, optimization, and compensation strategies. *Journal of Occupational Health Psychology 19*(1), 96.

Derue, D.S. and Ashford S.J. (2010). Who will lead and who will follow, a social process of leadership identity construction in organisations. *Academy of Management Review 35*(4), 627–647.

Dinh, J.E. and Lord, R.G. (2012). Implications of dispositional and process views of traits for individual difference research in leadership. *The Leadership Quarterly 23*(4), 651–669.

Doody, O., Slevin, E. and Taggart, L. (2012). Intellectual disability nursing in Ireland: Identifying its development and future. *Journal of Intellectual Disabilities 16*(1), 7–16.

Dulebohn, J.H., Bommer, W.H., Liden, R.C., Brouer, R.L. and Ferris, G.R. (2012). A meta-analysis of antecedents and consequences of leader-member exchange integrating the past with an eye toward the future. *Journal of Management 38*(6), 1715–1759.

Fletcher, J.K. (2004). The paradox of post heroic leadership: An essay on gender, power, and transformational change. *Leadership Quarterly 15*, 647–661.

Frankl, V.E. (1985). *Man's Search for Meaning*. New York, NY: Simon and Schuster.

Gagliardi, P. and Czarniawska, B. (2006). *Management Education and Humanities*. Northampton: Edward Elgar Publishing Inc.

Gardner, W.L., Avolio, B.J. and Walumbwa, F.O. (2005). Authentic leadership development: Emergent trends and future directions. In: W.L. Gardner, B.J. Avolio and F.O. Walumbwa (Eds.) *Authentic Leadership Theory and Practice: Origins, Effects, and Development*. Bingley: Emerald Group Publishing Ltd. pp. 387–406.

Gerstner, C.R. and Day, D.V. (1997). Meta-analytic review of leader-member exchange theory: Correlates and construct issues. *Journal of Applied Psychology 82*(6), 827.

Gronn, P. (2000). Distributed properties a new architecture for leadership. *Educational Management and Administration 28*(3), 317–338.

Gupta, V. and Singh, S. (2014). Psychological capital as a mediator of the relationship between leadership and creative performance behaviours: Empirical evidence from the Indian RandD sector. *The International Journal of Human Resource Management* 25(10), 1373–1394.

Health Service Executive (2012). *New Directions – Review of HSE Day Services and Implementation Plan 2012–2016.* Working Group Report. Dublin: HSE.

Higgs, M. and Dulewicz, V. (2014). Antecedents of well-being: A study to examine the extent to which personality and emotional intelligence contribute to well-being. *The International Journal of Human Resource Management* 25(5), 718–735.

Liao, H., Liu, D. and Loi, R. (2010). Looking at both sides of the social exchange coin: A social cognitive perspective on the joint effects of relationship quality and differentiation on creativity. *Academy of Management Journal* 53(5), 1090–1109.

Lines, B.C., Sullivan, K.T., Smithwick, J.B. and Mischung, J. (2015). Overcoming resistance to change in engineering and construction: Change management factors for owner organisations. *International Journal of Project Management* 33(5), 1170–1179.

Lück, M. (2011). An importance-performance analysis of backpackers at Robinson Crusoe Island resort, Fiji. *ARA Journal of Tourism Research* 3(1), 43–53.

Luthans, B.C., Luthans, K.W. and Avey, J.B. (2013). Building the leaders of tomorrow: The development of academic psychological capital. *Journal of Leadership and Organizational Studies* 21(2), 191–199.

Kielhofner, G. (2005). Rethinking disability and what to do about it: Disability studies and its implications for occupational therapy. *American Journal of Occupational Therapy* 59(5), 487–496.

Koys, D.J. (2001). The effects of employee satisfaction, organizational citizenship behavior, and turnover on organizational effectiveness: A unit-level, longitudinal study. *Personnel Psychology* 54(1), 101–114.

Mansell, J. and Beadle-Brown, J. (2012). *Active Support: Enabling and Empowering People Who Experience Intellectual Disabilities.* London: Jessica Kingsley Publishers.

McAlearney, A.S. (2006). Leadership development in healthcare: A qualitative study. *Journal of Organizational Behavior: The International Journal of Industrial, Occupational and Organizational Psychology and Behavior* 27(7), 967–982.

McConachie, D., McKenzie, K., Morris, P. and Walley, R. (2014). Acceptance and mindfulness-based stress management for support staff caring for individuals with intellectual disabilities. *Research in Developmental Disabilities* 35(6), 1216–1227.

Mengel, T. (2012). Leading with emotional intelligence – Existential and motivational analysis in leadership and leadership development. *Journal on Educational Psychology* 5(4), 24–31.

Montaño, D.E. and Kasprzyk, D. (2015). Theory of reasoned action, theory of planned behavior, and the integrated behavioral model. In: K. Glanz, B.K. Rimer and K. Viswanath (Eds.) *Health Behavior: Theory, Research, and Practice*. San Francisco, CA: Jossey-Bass. pp. 95–124.

Nadash, P. (1998). Independent choices. *American Rehabilitation* 24(3), 15–20.

Nadash, P. and Crisp, S. (2005). *Best Practices in Consumer Direction*. Washington, DC: Centers for Medicare and Medicaid Services.

Podsakoff, P.M. and MacKenzie, S.B. (1994). Organizational citizenship behaviors and sales unit effectiveness. *Journal of Marketing Research* 31(3), 351–363.

Power, A. (2013). Making space for belonging: Critical reflections on the implementation of personalised adult social care under the veil of meaningful inclusion. *Social Science and Medicine* 88, 68–75.

Reiss, S. (2008). *The Normal Personality: A New Way of Thinking about People*. Cambridge: Cambridge University Press.

Schalock, R.L. and Verdugo, M.A. (2012). *A Leadership Guide for Today's Disabilities Organizations: Overcoming Challenges and Making Change Happen*. Baltimore, MD: Brookes Publishing Company.

Schalock, R. and Verdugo, M. (2013). The transformation of disabilities organizations. *Intellectual and Developmental Disabilities* 51(4), 273–286.

Schaufeli, W.B. and Taris, T.W. (2014). *A Critical Review of the Job Demands-Resources Model: Implications for Improving Work and Health: Bridging Occupational, Organisational and Public Health*. Dordrecht: Springer.

Sinclair, A. (2005). *Doing Leadership Differently: Gender, Power and Sexuality in a Changing Business Culture*. Melbourne: Melbourne University Publishing.

Spillane, J.P. (2012). *Distributed Leadership*. (Vol. 4). London: John Wiley and Sons.

Stratman, J.K. and Roth, A.V. (2002). Enterprise resource planning (ERP) competence constructs: Two-stage multi-item scale development and validation. *Decision Sciences 33*(4), 601–628.

Swensen, S., Gorringe, G., Caviness, J. and Peters, D. (2016). Leadership by design: Intentional organization development of physician leaders. *Journal of Management Development 35*(4), 549–570.

Trichas, S. and Schyns, B. (2012). The face of leadership: Perceiving leaders from facial expression. *The Leadership Quarterly 23*(3), 545–566.

Truss, C., Shantz, A., Soane, E., Alfes, K. and Delbridge, R. (2013). Employee engagement, organisational performance and individual well-being: Exploring the evidence, developing the theory. *The International Journal of Human Resource Management 24*(14), 2657–2669.

Tugade, M.M., Fredrickson, B.L. and Feldman-Barrett, L. (2004). Psychological resilience and positive emotional granularity: Examining the benefits of positive emotions on coping and health. *Journal of Personality 72*(6), 1161–1190.

Van Dyne, L., Kossek, E. and Lobel, S. (2007). Less need to be there: Cross-level effects of work practices that support work-life flexibility and enhance group processes and group-level OCB. *Human Relations 60*(8), 1123–1154.

Wakabayashi, M., Chen, Z. and Graen, G.B. (2005). The global Asian way: Managerial efficacy profile (MEP) and LMX relationship in Asia. *LMX leadership: The Series. New Frontiers of Leadership 2*,121–137.

Xanthopoulou, D., Bakker, A.B., Demerouti, E. and Schaufeli, W.B. (2009). Reciprocal relationships between job resources, personal resources, and work engagement. *Journal of Vocational Behaviour 74*(3), 235–244.

Yamada, Y. (2001). Consumer direction in community-based long-term care: Implications for different stakeholders. *Journal of Gerontological Social Work 35*(3), 83–97.

Yukl, G. (2011). Contingency theories of effective leadership. *The SAGE Handbook of Leadership 24*(1), 286–298.

Zafar, F. and Naveed, K. (2014). Organizational change and dealing with employees' resistance. *International Journal of Management Excellence 2*(3), 237–246.

Chapter 5

The Psychology of Leadership

Christine Linehan

Contents

Chapter Topics

- ■ This chapter aims to explore the psychology of leadership by reviewing key models of leadership.
- ■ Theories reviewed in this chapter include:
  - – Great Man Theory
  - – Trait Theory
  - – Behavioural Approach
  - – Situational Approach
  - – Transactional and Transformational Leadership
  - – Authentic Leadership

Introduction

A myriad of pressures, ranging from local community advocacy groups through to the United Nation's Convention on the Rights of Persons with Disabilities, call for significant reform of the disability sector. Schalock and Verdugo (2012) observe that leaders within disability organisations must navigate this reform within the broader context of dwindling resources, increasing needs, workforce shortages, service fragmentation, quality issues, structural reconfiguration, public-private collaborations and increased requirements for governance within the sector. Faced with such challenges, it's regrettable but perhaps unsurprising, that the Irish Government referred to the pace of reform nationally as 'a slow and tentative drift towards individualised services' (Department of Health, 2012: 167).

Precisely how some jurisdictions have successfully navigated this reform, when others have not, has been the subject of both national and international research. In one US study, Parish (2005) explored disparity in the move towards individualised services in two Midwestern states. Closer to home, and one decade later, Linehan et al. (2015) sought to examine similar regional disparity in Ireland, again selecting two regions with differing progress towards individualised services. In both studies effective leadership was identified as a driver of reform; poor leadership stifled progress. In the Irish situation, those involved in the delivery and commissioning of services expressed their dissatisfaction with the lack of local and national leadership available to guide the implementation of policy. Their comments echo previous concerns noted in an evaluation of the implementation of personalised models of support throughout Europe which observed that in Ireland, 'the rhetoric does not match the reality. There is a vision, but no clear direction, leadership or mandate to put this into practice at local level' (Townsley et al., 2010: 16). Without appropriate leadership, both studies observed resistance to change and the paralysis of national policy.

The type of leaders required to drive innovation has been the study of many disciplines, psychology among them. Yet Warren Bennis, a pioneer of contemporary leadership, is uncompromising in his view that psychology has failed in its study of leadership. Bennis observed, in a special leadership edition of the prestigious academic journal *American Psychologist*

> To this day, psychologists have not sorted out which traits define leaders or whether leadership exists outside of specific situations, and yet we know with absolute certainty that a handful of people have changed millions of lives and reshaped the world.

(Bennis, 2007: 3)

The field of disability is no exception. History has shown that the lives of many individuals with disabilities were indeed changed by the actions of a small number of leaders in this field. Sir Francis Galton's scholarly leadership in the field of intelligence, for example, provided the impetus for the eugenics movement which advocated 'selective breeding' of the human race, with devastating consequences for people with disabilities. According to Bennis, herein lies an uncomfortable truth for psychologists; leadership must be viewed within the context of the leader's values. Perspectives on good or bad leadership include not only an objective assessment of the competencies of leaders' skills but also a subjective judgement of the moral compass of their leadership. Is a 'bad' leader one who is incompetent, immoral, or both? For psychologists who are trained in objective and scientific methods of enquiry, passing judgement on a leader's choice to act for ill or good may arguably conflict with psychology's scientific method. This conflict may explain why leadership research is more often found in business, public policy or educational courses than in the realm of psychology (Sternberg, 2007).

This chapter aims to explore the psychology of leadership by reviewing key models of leadership. These models, both theoretical and evidenced-based, reveal our evolving understanding of leaders and their complex interaction with followers and situations. Notwithstanding Bennis' critique of psychology's failure to develop a comprehensive theory of leadership, these interdisciplinary models attempt to offer some insight into the emergence and effectiveness of leaders, and in more recent years, how leaders engage with followers in an authentic manner to achieve shared goals.

Defining Leadership

Despite the collaborative and interdisciplinary nature of this field of study, no agreed definition of leadership exists among scholars. Rost (1991: 7) claims that 'over 60 percent of the authors who have written on leadership since about 1910 did not define leadership in their works'. Practitioners are equally criticised for defining leadership with an informal 'they know it when they see it'. These definitional challenges contribute to the contention that leadership may be something we recognise more by its absence than its presence.

Peter Northouse (2016), who authors the seminal textbook in the field *Leadership; Theory and Practice*, defines leadership as 'a process whereby an individual influences a group of individuals to achieve a common goal' (2016: 6). By defining leadership as a process, Northouse dislodges a key element of many people's understanding of leadership, the assumption that leadership is a trait or cluster of characteristics bestowed on individuals. For Northouse, leadership is conceptualised as a dynamic interaction between leaders and followers. Without followers to be influenced, Northouse argues there can be no leaders. This definition echoes that of Rost (1991) who described leaders and followers as two sides of the same coin.

Within an organisational setting, the process of leadership should be distinguished from that of management. Kotter (1990) describes management as a process of planning, budgeting, staffing and problem solving. This can be contrasted with leadership which, according to Schalock and Verdugo (2012), is a process of inspiring people and organisations to change, and more specifically 'to want to change'. For Schalock and Verdugo, leadership in disability organisations involves all personnel including CEO, management and direct support staff. The disability sector, however, and the reform needed to align with a more inclusive and rights-based approach, extends beyond individual disability organisations to include an array of stakeholders such as individuals with disabilities, advocates, caregivers, natural community supports, commissioners, practitioners and policy makers. How one individual might exert sufficient influence over multiple stakeholders to achieve long-standing change has been explored in a variety of models, the more salient of which are presented in this chapter.

Great Man Theory

Credited to works such as Thomas Carlyle's 1841 publication *On Heroes, Hero-Worship, and the Heroic in History* and Sir Francis Galton's 1892 publication *Hereditary Genius*, the Great Man Theory of leadership argues that leaders are born, not made. Observation of great men throughout history led these theorists to conclude that leadership is destined from birth. Each hero merely has to await his, rarely her, moment to rise above the mundane and reveal his full potential. The theory has a seductive charm for all who can recall their childhood hero and differentiate the qualities that mark this hero apart from others. Their leadership is characterised by individuals who are superior and special, exuding a quality that epitomises leadership as a phenomenon where followers 'know it when they see it'. One elusive trait more than most encapsulates what it is to be a Great Man, that of charisma. Weber (1922, as cited in Haslam et al., 2011) defines charisma as comprising divine, magical and superhuman qualities. The assumption that these traits are present from birth, and pass from one generation to the next, limits positions of leadership to the preserve of a few Great Men (Zaccaro, 2007) and, in present day situations, may result in some individuals being unquestionably raised to positions of leadership.

Trait Theory

By the 1930s to the 1950s, Trait Theory, a variant of the Great Man theory, dominated the study of leadership. Trait theory aimed to enumerate which specific qualities or traits, whether innate or acquired, distinguish leaders from non-leaders. Exploiting the potential of large population-based psychometric studies which gathered vast amounts of information on personality traits of the general population, trait theory sought to determine whether the characteristics of individuals in general, rather than of a few select individuals, can predict leadership. Two seminal reviews of such studies were published by Stogdill in 1948 and Mann in 1959. Stogdill's review of 124 studies published in the *Journal of Psychology* aimed to explore the predictive relationship between 27 traits and leadership, albeit Stogdill noted that many studies failed to state how precisely they defined leadership. Eight traits were identified as being predictive of leadership; intelligence, alertness, insight, responsibility, initiative, persistence, self-confidence and sociability. While the temptation was to assume individuals with these skills would engage in effective leadership, Stogdill had to acknowledge that the strength of the predictive relationship was weak and that the findings across studies were variable and inconsistent. Stogdill concluded that leadership must comprise more than the mere characteristics of leaders, commenting, 'it becomes clear that an adequate analysis of leadership involves not only a study of leaders but also of situations' (Stogdill, 1948: 64–65).

Mann (1959) conducted a similar review over a decade later, exploring the relationship between leadership and seven personality dimensions which were assessed by over 500 different measures. The seven personality dimensions were intelligence, adjustment, extraversion-introversion, dominance, masculinity-femininity, conservatism and interpersonal sensitivity. Within the papers selected for review, leadership was operationalised in four ways; as rated by observers, as rated by peers, as rated by an individual's formal office, and as self-rated. The strongest positive association reported with leadership was intelligence, with other positive associations being reported for adjustment, extraversion, dominance, masculinity and interpersonal sensitivity. A negative association was reported between leadership and conservatism. Similar to Stogdill's findings, however, these relationships were weak, with the strongest relationship, that of intelligence and leadership, revealing that just 5% of the variation in leadership could be explained by intelligence.

Mann concluded, like Stogdill, that the relationship observed between traits and leadership was mediated by context; that is, the possession of traits which contributed to an individual exhibiting leadership in one situation would not automatically result in the individual demonstrating leadership in a different situation. This finding may be beneficial in the current reconfiguration of disability services as a reminder that while certain individuals may excel in demonstrating leadership skills in one arena, the temptation to automatically assume these individuals will excel in other arenas, potentially resulting in their ascendency within an organisation, should be both recognised and carefully considered; effective leadership is not necessary a transferable skill.

Despite the intrinsic appeal that leadership can be successfully predicted by individual characteristics, the model is challenged by its logical conclusion that individuals who fail to possess certain characteristics are incapable of exercising effective leadership. The model is also challenged by its assumption that leadership is associated with fixed traits, a position that fails to explain how leaders are observed to develop and grow into their leadership roles. Perhaps most damning, however, is the evidence of a weak predictive relationship between traits and leadership; contrary to the common perception, leaders are more likely made than born.

Behavioural Approach

As the name suggests, behaviourist theories of leadership seek to define leadership in terms of leaders' behaviours rather than their characteristics. Dominating many fields of psychology throughout the 1950s and 1960s, behaviourism offered a new perspective to the leadership debate. Are certain behaviours predictive of effective leadership? If so, can these behaviours, and by implication leadership, be taught?

Pioneering studies by Fleishman (1953) and Fleishman and Peters (1962) surveyed leaders in industry, education and military fields. Approximately 2,000 behaviours were identified from which the researchers developed the Leadership Behaviour Description Questionnaire (LBDQ). The LBDQ is a questionnaire which employees complete on behalf of their supervisor. Typical of a myriad of tools now available to assess

leadership styles, the questionnaire requires employees to
consider how frequently their supervisor engages in an array
of different behaviours. From their responses, the supervisor's
leadership style is determined. These tools provide an opportunity for those in leadership roles to understand and reflect
on how their leadership is appraised by others, potentially in
both directions by sub- and super-ordinates.

The LBDQ-XII, developed by Stogdill (1974), is a revised
version of the LBDQ and is considered one of the most
widely used leadership questionnaires. It identifies two
main categories of leadership styles; one style of leadership
prioritises the leader's consideration of employees, termed
'consideration', the other prioritises the leader's engagement
in maximising productivity, termed 'initiation of structure'.
These two leadership styles are well evidenced across a
variety of contexts (Katz and Kahn, 1951; Kahn, 1956; Blake
and Mouton, 1964). While some theorists argue these styles
represent two ends of a continuum, with leaders being either
employee or production focused, the weight of evidence is
that they comprise two independent concepts and consequently leaders may engage in both, one, or neither styles
(Northouse, 2016).

Path-goal theory explores whether particular leadership
styles are more effective in some situations than others. In
general, the evidence suggests that where a task is unclear,
complex and being undertaken by followers who may be
resistant to change, a focus on 'initiation of structure' may
be more beneficial as it provides clear and structured guidance to these followers. In contrast, in situations where tasks
are repetitive and are undertaken by employees who may
feel unchallenged and undervalued, a focus on consideration
in supporting employees may be more appropriate (House
and Mitchell, 1974). Within the content of significant reform
within the disability sector, consideration is required as to how
best the implementation of new practices and policies may
be successfully introduced. What are the needs of followers

who may feel resistant, unchallenged or undervalued? What
are the characteristics of followers charged with implementation and what leadership supports may optimise successful
implementation?

The behaviourist approach to leadership suffers the same
criticism as that levelled at Trait Theory; that the model fails
to provide a universal model of leadership given there is
little consensus on which behaviours guarantee optimal outcomes across tasks and followers. Notwithstanding this criticism, there is a strong evidence-base behind this approach
which has contributed to the development of an array of
measurement tools and management training programmes. By
definition, these training programmes reflect an underlying
assumption that leadership can be taught.

Situational Approach

Does leadership emerge in particular situations? An extreme
position addressing this question would argue that any individual may emerge as a leader if the situation demands it. Haslam
et al. (2011) cite Prof Zimbardo's Stanford Prison Experiment
as an example. This experiment randomly allocated a sample
of undergraduate students to the roles of guards and prisoners in a simulated prison environment. Mindful that the prison
was a simulation, both parties unexpectedly embraced their
roles as if the situation was real. The guards, in particular,
engaged in cruel and punitive punishment of prisoners. Within
days, the safety of participants in the experiment became
of such concern that the research was terminated. For the
researchers, the behaviour of the guards was deemed a natural
consequence when assuming a position of authority; personal
agency was overwhelmed by situation.

A less absolute position is that leadership is influenced
in part by the situation. A seminal work here is Fiedler's

Contingency Theory which pioneered the notion that leadership effectiveness reflects an interaction between leaders' traits and the situation. Leaders are more effective if their style fits the situation, in particular, if they are respected by followers, if the task structure aligns with their leadership style, and if the leader has sufficient power over followers to implement goals. More recently, the Situational Leadership model (Blanchard et al., 2013) suggests that leaders provide followers with different levels of direction (prioritising productivity) and support (prioritising employees), based on an appraisal of the situation and the needs of their followers. Leadership styles include directing, coaching, supporting and delegating; each dependent on the leader's appraisal of followers' level of competency and motivation. Early stage followers, for example, are typically high on motivation yet, given their inexperience, are low on competency. With experience, they develop competencies, albeit with lower motivation if some of the initial glow of the task wanes. In contrast, more experienced followers may engage in high levels of both competency and motivation to complete a task.

In order for leaders to be effective, the situational approach to leadership proposes that leaders must successfully determine the developmental level of their followers and adjust their own leadership style to optimally suit this level. Within the context of a major reconfiguration of the disability sector, this model of leadership suggests that the developmental stage of followers should be considered, and that those in positions of leadership should be supported to accurately assess and purposefully respond to the needs of their followers.

The situational approach to leadership provides a valuable contribution in recognising the role of context in our understanding of leadership. It also provides frameworks for guiding leaders on how different leadership styles impact on different situations, which has application for leadership training programmes.

Transactional and Transformational Leadership

Transactional and transformational leadership styles were originally identified as part of universal leadership theories identifying three core leadership styles; transactional, transformational and laissez-faire (Burns, 1978; Bass, 1985). Transactional and transformational leadership styles have been extensively examined, less so the laissez-faire style which, by definition, represents the absence of leadership.

Based on earlier works by Max Weber (1947), transactional leadership, also termed Exchange Theory, is characterised by a transaction between leaders and followers. Transactional leaders typically hold formal positions of authority within organisations, where distinct work plans are developed for employees and production conforms to pre-existing regulations. An example is a factory supervisor who is responsible for ensuring a specified number of products are completed, to a given standard, within a given timeframe. Productivity is the core goal, irrespective of employees' motivation or opinion on how productivity may be enhanced. The transaction is undertaken by the leader bestowing followers with rewards (e.g., pay) or punishment (e.g., dismissal) contingent on their productivity. Productivity is monitored by a corrective management style, termed Management by Exception, where management personnel become involved only in situations where productivity deviates from expected performance; generally, production should run like clockwork. Managers may differ in the degree of monitoring and intervention they engage in; an 'active' style is described for those who expect and respond to minor deviations in performance, while a 'passive' style is represented by managers who respond only in cases where serious deviations from expected performance arise. Irrespective of the level of engagement in responding to deviation, at the heart of the transactional leadership style is a simple exchange, with one party having authority to reward or punish the other for their level of productivity. This exchange metaphor, however, fails to recognise, or harness, the motivation, creativity and agency of followers. In times of economic austerity, a follower may remain in a monotonous and unfulfilling role for the reward of a much-needed salary. These same followers, in times where work options are more plentiful, may, however, find the exchange unrewarding and simply look elsewhere (Haslam et al., 2011).

Transformational leaders provide a stark contrast to transactional leaders. As the name suggests, these leaders transform their followers by inspiring them to support a shared vision beyond their own interest (Judge and Piccolo, 2004). Reminiscent of the era of the Great Men, James McGregor Burns developed the concept of transformational leadership following a qualitative analysis of political leaders. While Burns classified transformational leaders as a distinct group from transactional leaders, Bernard Bass extended his work and envisaged the two styles as complementary rather than opposing. Transformational styles may be ineffective in the absence of a transactional understanding of which tasks must be undertaken, and for what reward (Bass et al., 1987). A middle ground is the 'augmentation hypothesis' which proposes that a transformational leader may require support from a transactional leader to ensure that vision is translated into outcome (Tosi, 1982). Someone needs to ensure that the innovative, creative and visionary guidance provided by transformational leaders produces results.

Transactional and transformational styles can be measured using the Multifactor Leadership Questionnaire (MLQ);(Bass, 1985; Bass et al., 1987) which was developed by asking 70 executives to describe traits of transactional and transformational leaders. The MLQ is now deemed the seminal measure of these leadership types. As measured by the MLQ, transformational leaders are defined by Idealised Influence (or Charisma), Inspirational Motivation, Individual Consideration and Intellectual Stimulation. Charisma instils pride and loyalty among followers. Inspirational Motivation is the degree to which leaders share a vision which is appealing to followers and motivates them to achieve future goals to high standards. Individualised Consideration is observed when leaders treat their followers with respect and provide opportunities for growth which results in followers feeling trust, loyalty and respect for the leader. Intellectual Stimulation is provided through encouraging followers to be innovative while engaging in reasoned problem solving. The impact of this transformational leadership is that followers achieve outputs beyond those originally envisaged. They are motivated not by personal gain, but by an inspired and shared vision. In a contrasting style, the MLQ defines transactional leaders as those engaging in Contingent Reward (rewards are provided contingent on output) and Management by Exception (existing practices remain in place unless proven problematic). A comprehensive review of research using the MLQ reported a strong association between effectiveness in leadership and the transformational scales, with Charisma being consistently the most strongly related characteristic related to effective leadership (Lowe et al., 1996). In contrast, some transactional leadership styles have a weak relationship with leadership effectiveness; in particular, Management by Exception has almost no relationship with effectiveness.

Northouse identifies a number of strengths to this model of leadership, notably the strong evidence of effectiveness for transformational leadership (Yukl, 1999). Such is the popularity of transformational leadership, that it comprised 34% of all academic articles published from 1990 to 2000 in the prestigious journal *Leadership Quarterly* (Northouse, 2016). The success of the model is not only its strong evidence-base and intuitive appeal but for some its moral dimension. Northouse comments that 'this emphasis sets the transformational approach apart from all other approaches to leadership because it suggests that leadership has a moral dimension' (Northouse, 2016: 177).

Where there are strengths, there are weaknesses, and transformation leadership does not escape the latter. It may, for example, be seen to be elitist, with an unquestioning faith in the vision of the leader. The charismatic quality of the leader contributes to this perception, where transformational leadership and charisma as terms are used interchangeably.

Moreover, for leaders who equate their transformational style with the undefined mystical quality that is charisma, there is a possibility that they will become autocratic and intolerant of dissent (Yukl, 1999). Evidence of those in leadership position wielding their power in this way has spawned interest in the 'dark side' of leadership, asking how some individuals follow leaders to the precipice and beyond (Tourish, 2013).

Authentic Leadership

Responding to a perceived decrease in ethical leadership, as witnessed in a series of economic scandals and the rise of terrorist-related fundamentalism, Authentic Leadership is an emerging area in leadership which seeks to identify genuine leaders who are trusted by followers to bring certainty within the context of a shared moral code. Proponents aim to train and develop leaders who will behave in ways which are deemed ethically and socially responsible (Cooper et al., 2005). Authentic leaders are described as being self-aware of their values, goals, strengths and weaknesses; being driven by the desire to make a difference; maintaining objectivity in their perspective; and demonstrating an ability to reveal themselves to others in a transparent and open manner. Mindful of the lack of consensus in definitions of Authentic Leadership, Avolio et al. (2004a), define authentic leaders as

> those who are deeply aware of how they think and behave and are perceived by others as being of their own and others' values/moral perspectives, knowledge and strengths; aware of the context in which they operate; and who are confident, hopeful, optimistic, resilient, and of high moral character.
>
> **(Avolio et al., 2004b: 4)**

At issue for current theorists is the conceptual overlap between Authentic Leadership and Transformational

Leadership. Are the two forms of leadership truly distinct? Does any overlap between them warrant one conceptually redundant? A recent meta-analysis compared studies involving over 25,000 individuals exploring these two types of leadership (Banks et al., 2016). The study found that authentic leadership and transformational leadership are strongly related and therefore a degree of redundancy is undoubtedly present. There is, however, a difference in the ability of the two types of leadership to predict outcomes. Transformation Leadership is associated with high levels of job performance, task performance, satisfaction with leadership and leadership effectiveness. In contrast, Authentic Leadership is associated with high levels of organisational performance and organisational citizenship behaviours, the latter being defined as employees' voluntary commitments within an organisation which exceed the boundaries of their contractual obligations. For Banks et al. (2016) the difference reflects the salient outcome of each type of leadership. Transformational leadership inspires followers to attain exceptional levels of performance. This focus likely explains the high levels of satisfaction reported by these followers with both their job and their leader. In contrast, the ethical and moral focus of Authentic Leadership encourages followers to support the collective more so than individual attainment. For this reason, these followers prioritise the broader aspects of organisational rather than individual performance, engaging in voluntary activities beneficial to the organisation and outside the scope of their personal contract.

Authentic leadership is in the early stages of development, and aspects of the theory require further clarification and research. In particular, the suggestion that leaders are motivated by a higher moral dimension requires further clarity (Northouse, 2016). What is clear, however, is evidence that Authentic Leadership is associated with an inhibition by followers to engage in unethical choices (Cianci et al., 2014); a finding which will resonate with many in the disability sector following revelations of scandal and abuse among those delivering support services.

Conclusions

What conclusions regarding the psychology of leadership might be drawn from key leadership approaches? Leaders are more likely made than born. While intelligence is associated with effective leadership, it is moderately so; other traits that may traditionally be deemed indicative of leadership, such as self-confidence and dominance, are in fact weakly related. In exercising leadership, individuals typically prioritise either followers or tasks, and this prioritisation may vary depending on the characteristics of the task at hand and the situation. Leaders need to determine these characteristics and modify their leadership style accordingly whether coaching, delegating or using some other leadership style.

More recently, attention has focused on the transformational influence and authenticity of leaders. The moral component of these models, a feature which Bennis may argue might further alienate psychologists, aligns with the near universal adoption of a rights-based and personalised approach to disability. The reconfiguration of services requires a clear vision of the future, as articulated in international charters such as the United Nation's Convention on the Rights of Persons with Disabilities which has now filtered to many national level policies in areas such as deinstitutionalisation and personalisation.

This new vision has been honed by the contributions of many transformational, charismatic leaders such as Judith Heumann, the World Bank's first adviser on disability, Mike Oliver who first coined the term 'social model of disability' and John O'Brien who pioneered personal centred planning, to name but a few. These visionary individuals have undoubtedly transformed the disability landscape. Armed with a clear vision of what the future may aspire to, the disability sector must consider not only this vision but, in addition, the journey to implementation. The bridge from vision to implementation is where many will experience challenges and effective leadership is an imperative for success (Schalock and Verdugo, 2012).

These challenges are perhaps unsurprising given the questionable portrayal of a hierarchy where policy typically directs leadership, which in turn directs on the ground activities (Linehan et al., 2015). In reality, those charged with articulating a vision at national and local levels are most likely government and senior figures within disability organisations. Those responsible for implementation are more typically organisational managers who introduce system-level changes, such as training, recruitment and staff conditions. Those involved in actual implementation, delivering change in person-to-person interactions, are typically people with disabilities, their families and staff. Effective leadership is needed to translate the chosen vision through organisational systems to the end point of optimal person-to-person interaction. For Schalock and Verdugo (2012) organisation change often fails because 'leaders and managers have failed to change the deeply ingrained assumptions, generalisations and images that help organisation personnel understand the world and experience (or visualise) the future' (Schalock and Verdugo, 2012: 6). These deeply ingrained assumptions are as likely held by individuals with disabilities and their families as they are by staff working in disability services. Leadership is needed to drive innovative and sustainable reform that is agreed and advocated for by all stakeholder groups. Arriving at this position requires 'a process whereby an individual influences a group of individuals to achieve a common goal', a journey Northouse (2016) describes as leadership.

Key Concepts Discussed

- Great Man Theory
- Trait Theory
- Behavioural Approach
- Situational Approach
- Transactional and Transformational Leadership
- Authentic Leadership

Key Readings

- Alilyyani, B., Wong, C. A. and Cummings, G. (2018).
  Antecedents, mediators, and outcomes of authentic leadership in healthcare: A systematic review. *International
  Journal of Nursing Studies 83*, 34–64.
  Systematic review of 21 papers which describe authentic leadership in healthcare settings. Data extraction
  sought to identify associations between authentic leadership and antecedents, mediators and outcomes. The paper
  presents an adapted authentic leadership model emanating from these relationships.
- Greenhalgh, T., Robert, G., Macfarlane, F., Bate, P. and
  Kyriakidou, O. (2004). Diffusion of innovations in service
  organisations: systematic review and recommendations.
  The Milbank Quarterly 82(4), 581–629.
  This highly cited article presents findings from a
  systematic review of innovations in the health care
  sector. Leadership is included as one of a number of
  key areas which influence the introduction of these
  innovations.
- Laschinger, H. K. S., Wong, C. A. and Grau, A. L.
  (2012). The influence of authentic leadership on newly
  graduated nurses' experiences of workplace bullying, burnout and retention outcomes: A cross-sectional
  study. *International Journal of Nursing Studies 49*(10),
  1266–1276.
  This research paper explores the influence of authentic
  leadership on the work environment of 342 newly graduated nurses and concludes that authentic leadership promotes job retention by decreasing bullying and burnout
  rates and increasing job satisfaction.
- Northouse, P. G. (2016). *Leadership: Theory and practice.*
  (7th edition). Thousand Oaks, CA: Sage Publications.
  Now in its 7th edition, this is the definitive textbook
  in leadership studies. Citing research evidence for a wide

array of leadership models, the textbook also includes case studies and a self-assessment questionnaire.

■ Schalock, R. L. and Verdugo, M. A. (2012). *A Leadership Guide for Today's Disabilities Organizations: Overcoming Challenges and Making Change Happen*. Baltimore: Brookes Publishing Company.

An innovative textbook providing a how-to guide for organisational change. The book combines academic research with practical application. Eight approaches to change are reviewed, with actionable steps and reflective worksheets.

■ Tafvelin, S., Armelius, K. and Westerberg, K. (2011). Toward understanding the direct and indirect effects of transformational leadership on well-being: A longitudinal study. *Journal of Leadership and Organizational Studies* *18*(4), 480–492.

Longitudinal study of 158 care assistants, social workers and nurses from a large social service organisation in Sweden. At both Time 1, and 12 months later at Time 2, well-being of employees was predicted by a climate of innovation, which in turn was predicted by transformational leadership. The authors conclude that transformational leaders contribute to employee well-being by creating a climate characterised by encouragement to make improvements, possibilities to exercise initiative and encourage communication.

Useful Websites

■ Leadership in the History of the Developmental Disabilities Movement http://www.disabilityhistorywiki.org/leadership/
■ The National Leadership Consortium on Developmental Disabilities http://www.nlcdd.org/

References

Avolio, B. J., Gardner, W. L., Walumbwa, F. O., Luthans, F. and May, D. R. (2004a). Unlocking the mask: A look at the process by which authentic leaders impact follower attitudes and behaviors. *The Leadership Quarterly 15*(6), 801–823.

Avolio, B., Luthans, F. and Walumbwa, F. O. (2004b). *Authentic Leadership: Theory-Building for Veritable Sustained Performance.* Working paper. Lincoln, NB: Gallup Leadership Institute, University of Nebraska.

Banks, G. C., McCauley, K. D., Gardner, W. L. and Guler, C. E. (2016). A meta-analytic review of authentic and transformational leadership: A test for redundancy. *The Leadership Quarterly 27*(4), 634–652.

Bass, B. M. (1985). *Leadership and Performance beyond Expectations.* New York, NY: Free Press.

Bass, B. M., Avolio, B. J. and Goodheim, L. (1987). Biography and the assessment of transformational leadership at the world-class level. *Journal of Management 13*(1), 7–19.

Bennis, W. (2007). The challenges of leadership in the modern world: Introduction to the special issue. *American Psychologist 62*(1), 2.

Blake, R.R., & Mouton, J.S. (1964). *The Managerial Grid.* Houston, TX: Gulf Publishing Company.

Blanchard, K., Zigarmi, P. and Zigarmi, D. (2013). *Leadership and the One Minute Manager: Increasing Effectiveness through Situational Leadership II.* New York, NY: William Morrow.

Burns, J. M. (1978). *Leadership.* New York, NY: Harper and Row.

Cianci, A.M., Hannah, S.T., Roberts, R.P., and Tsakumis, G.T. (2014). The effects of authentic leadership on followers' ethical decision-making in the face of temptation: An experimental study. *The Leadership Quarterly*, 25, 581–594.

Cooper, C. D., Scandura, T. A. and Schriesheim, C. A. (2005). Looking forward but learning from our past: Potential challenges to developing authentic leadership theory and authentic leaders. *The Leadership Quarterly 16*(3), 475–493.

Department of Health (2012). *Value for Money and Policy Review of Disability Services in Ireland.* Dublin: Department of Health.

Fleishman, E. A. (1953). The description of supervisory behavior. *Journal of Applied Psychology 37*(1), 1.

Fleishman, E. A. and Peters, D. R. (1962). Interpersonal values, leadership attitudes, and managerial "success". *Personnel Psychology 15*(2), 127–143.

Haslam, S. A., Reicher, S. D. and Platow, M. J. (2011). *The New Psychology of Leadership: Identity, Influence and Power.* Sussex: Psychology Press.

House, R.J., & Mitchell, R.R. (1974). Path-goal theory of leadership. *Journal of Contemporary Business*, 3, 81–97.

Judge, T. A. and Piccolo, R. F. (2004). Transformational and transactional leadership: A meta-analytic test of their relative validity. *Journal of Applied Psychology 89*(5), 755.

Kahn, R. L. (1956). The prediction of productivity. *Journal of Social Issues 12*, 41–49.

Katz, D. and Kahn, R. L. (1951). Human organization and worker motivation. In: L. R. Tripp (Ed.) *Industrial Productivity.* Madison, WI: Industrial Relations Research Association. pp. 146–171.

Kotter, J. P. (1990). *A Force for Change: How Leadership Differs from Management.* New York, NY: Free Press.

Linehan, C., O'Doherty, S., Tatlow-Golden, M., Craig, S., Kerr, M., Lynch, C., McConkey, R. and Staines, A. (2015). *Moving Ahead. Factors Contributing to the Successful Transition of People with Intellectual Disabilities from Congregated to Community-Based Residential Options in Two Regions in Ireland.* Dublin: School of Social Work and Social Policy, Trinity College Dublin.

Lowe, K. B., Kroeck, K. G. and Sivasubramaniam, N. (1996). Effectiveness correlates of transformational and transactional leadership: A meta-analytic review of the MLQ literature. *The Leadership Quarterly 7*(3), 385–425.

Mann, R. D. (1959). Personal factors associated with leadership: A survey of the literature. *Journal of Psychology 25*, 241–270.

Northouse, P. G. (2016). *Leadership: Theory and Practice* (7th edition). Thousand Oaks, CA: Sage Publications.

Parish, S. L. (2005). Deinstitutionalization in two states: The impact of advocacy, policy, and other social forces on services for people with developmental disabilities. *Research and Practice for Persons with Severe Disabilities 30*(4), 1–13.

Rost, J. C. (1991). *Leadership for the Twenty-first Century.* New York, NY: Praeger.

Schalock, R. L. and Verdugo, M. A. (2012). *A Leadership Guide for Today's Disabilities Organizations: Overcoming Challenges and Making Change Happen*. Baltimore, MD: Brookes Publishing Company.

Sternberg, R. J. (2007). A systems model of leadership: WICS. *American Psychologist 62*(1), 34.

Stogdill, R. M. (1948). Personal factors associated with leadership: A survey of the literature. *The Journal of Psychology 25*(1), 35–71.

Stogdill, R. M. (1974). *Handbook of Leadership: A Survey of Theory and Research*. New York, NY: Free Press.

Tosi Jr., H. (1982). Toward a paradigm shift in the study of leadership. In: J. G. Hunt, U. Sekaran and C. A. Schriescheim (Eds.) *Leadership: Beyond Establishment Views*. Carbondale, IL: Southern Illinois University Press. pp. 222–223.

Tourish, D. (2013). The dark side of transformational leadership: A critical perspective. *Industrial and Commercial Training 45*(6), 369–370.

Townsley, R., Ward, L., Abbott, D. and Williams, V. (2010). *Implementation of Policies Supporting Independent Living for Disabled People in Europe: Synthesis Report. Academy Network of European Disability Experts (ANED)*. Bristol: Norah Fry Research Centre.

Weber, M. (1947). *The Theory of Social and Economic Organisations*. New York: Oxford University Press.

Yukl, G. (1999). An evaluation of conceptual weaknesses in transformational and charismatic leadership theories. *The Leadership Quarterly 10*(2), 285–305.

Zaccaro, S. J. (2007). Trait-based perspectives of leadership. *American Psychologist 62*(1), 6.

INNOVATING THROUGH CHANGE

Chapter 6

Beyond Controversy in Change Management? Rethinking Options for Intellectual Disability Services

Martin Beirne

Contents

Chapter Topics

- **Contextual pressures for change in Intellectual Disability Service (IDS)**
- **Opportunities and dilemmas in change management**
- **Critical scrutiny of common assumptions and popular prescriptions**
- **A reappraisal of the foundational scholarship of Kurt Lewin**
- **Principle-driven progress rather than top-down managerialism**
- **Participative and empowering approaches to achieving necessary, viable and appreciated forms of organisational change**

Introduction

There is a clamour for change in intellectual disability services. After revelations about care failures and shortfalls in provision similar to those stimulating change in other areas of healthcare (BBC, 2012; O'Mahony, 2014), fresh priorities have been set, with attention firmly focused on core principles that should influence practical reforms and provide essential criteria for evaluating the success (or otherwise) of change initiatives. Respect, inclusion and empowerment are key watchwords in this, with explicit calls for more person-centred policies and practices emanating from a swathe of official and critical review documentation, notably in Britain

and Ireland (Department of Health, 2001; Transforming
Care and Commissioning Steering Group Report, 2014; UK
Strengthening the Commitment Steering Group, 2015). Change
is to be managed in ways that enable recipients and providers of care – patients, their families and responsible front line
staff – to have more of a say and much greater influence on
quality, well-being and the everyday experiences of the people who rely on intellectual disability services.

The scale of change required to deliver on this agenda is
widely acknowledged, with broad-ranging and often creative
proposals for skills development, competency frameworks,
statements of rights and responsibilities and institutional support structures presented to governments and health authorities (UK Strengthening the Commitment Steering Group, 2015).
That said, what is to be achieved is rather more obvious in
much of this deliberation than how the various stakeholders
can devise operational initiatives that are capable of securing
and sustaining meaningful improvements. Despite references
to established business and social science literature on change
management, there is a dearth of critical knowledge about
the limitations of much conventional theory and practice in
this area, and an evident propensity among health professionals to endorse, or slip unreflectively towards, the application
of less empowering approaches to management and work
organisation.

This chapter considers ways forward for change management in intellectual disability services, setting out key principles and practical possibilities while urging caution about the
quality of available advice, the effectiveness of well-publicised
interventions and the claims emanating from the consultancy
community, which are frequently inflated and unrealistic. The
theoretical and practical lessons that can be drawn from critical and alternative sources will be examined and applied to
the management of opportunities and constraints within the
intellectual disability service sector.

The Change Management Orthodoxy

When looking for practical means of achieving change in times of crisis or difficulty, it is understandable that practitioners should turn to established literature and popular techniques. Change management is far from a settled subject, however, and has been blighted by a proliferation of decontextualised dictums, unrealistic yet oft-repeated assertions, crude oversimplifications, trite statements of technique, and regular bouts of sloganising about heroic ways of overcoming irrational resistance (Collins, 1998; Sturdy and Grey, 2003). This is recognised in at least part of the IDS literature, with complaints recorded about the trade in jargon, simplistic models and formulaic lists (Callaly and Arya, 2005). Clinicians are concerned that healthcare managers are too easily seduced by superficial prescriptions, adopting a 'plug-in' approach to their implementation with little obvious appreciation of professional priorities and dilemmas (Davidson, 2015).

Despite this awareness, there is still a tendency to rely on orthodox change management (OCM), to entertain the possibility that the underpinnings are safe and to trust that the unpalatable elements exist alongside useful knowledge that should be part of every change agents 'tool box' (Davidson, 2015). This section highlights the danger of taking too much for granted with OCM. Since the problems with prescriptive theory and practice have been well rehearsed over many years, it suggests that healthcare commentators are unduly receptive to some spurious assumptions about 'good change management' (Varkey and Antonio, 2010; Davidson, 2015), and also curiously reluctant to explore alternative possibilities. By magnifying key weaknesses, including the selective (mis)interpretation of influential social science contributions within the development of OCM, this section begins to make the case for greater confidence in following through on critical inclinations and reimagining what change management, or leadership, really requires and involves.

An important initial point to make is that change is necessary in healthcare, including IDS, to address a legacy of inadequate leadership and poor management. This relates to established principles and preoccupations that reveal an explicit logic of approach, and is not just attributable to the failings of particular individuals or groups. Orthodox notions of 'leaderism' (O'Reilly and Reed, 2010) and managerialism (Sturdy and Grey, 2003) have been linked to serious care failures and shortfalls in performance that are patterned rather than isolated or localised, and which call attention to the insularity of managerial hierarchies and a directive rationale that is geared to efficiency rather than effectiveness (Francis, 2013; Keogh, 2013).

The core assumptions of OCM produce similar tendencies and problems, beginning with the prescriptive certainty that organisational change needs to be carefully handled, independently analysed and purposefully influenced, shaped or controlled by rational, objective change agents. Even change that is unanticipated, emergent and spontaneous must be directed or redirected to deliver organisational advantage, with the expertise of rational managers establishing what this means in practice.

This characteristic drive to control change and promote a mechanistic understanding of managerial leverage on or over it is typically traced to the foundational work of Kurt Lewin and his classic three-step model of unfreezing, moving and refreezing (Callaly and Arya, 2005). Appreciative accounts of the 'Lewin three-step' helped to define the role of change agents in the prescriptive literature, ostensibly providing a powerful tool to guide managerial interventions (Levasseur, 2001). With an image of the forces that enable and inhibit useful change counterbalancing each other, considered management intervention is evidently needed to disrupt the status quo, implement an appropriate change programme and then fix it in place as the new settled state. In this way, rational management control is installed at the centre of change theory and practice. The history of OCM is then presented as a trajectory of measured progress towards the current 'state of the art', with subsequent applications of systems thinking and rational interventionism building on the Lewin foundations to equip managers with more refined n-step guides (Collins, 1998; Kotter, 1996; Callaly and Arya, 2005) and supposedly more sophisticated techniques to engineer official or legitimate change.

This storyline is regularly reproduced in the management literature, although there is now an established counter-history that links criticism and corrective to alternative principles and possibilities for leading and managing change (Cummings et al., 2016; Burnes et al., 2018). The poverty of managerial writing about Lewin is at the heart of this. Indeed, the extent to which Lewin's work is misinterpreted and misunderstood is taken as confirmation of the crudity of OCM and its inadequacy as a guide to action.

Lewin's applied social science was far richer and more inclusive than contemporary managerial accounts suggest (Burnes, 2004; Beirne, 2008). Certainly, he was engaged in applied scholarship, although this was informed by humanistic and democratic values that were forged through his personal experiences with anti-Semitism and German Nationalism. His approach was based on a strong ethical commitment to participation and mutual learning, and this was channelled into a practical agenda that addressed problems of racism, conflict and disadvantage within and beyond work organisations. Consequently, most of the recent scholarship on Lewin's contribution connect it to group dynamics, action research and a vision of change that is not reducible to prescriptive managerialism. There are doubts about the importance that Lewin himself attached to the three-step imagery, and some compelling lines of argument that it was rigidified through reworking and populist repackaging after his death (Cummings et al., 2016).

A deeper and more sensitive reading of Lewin's applied research broadens the value base for framing and evaluating change initiatives, and extends the list of stakeholders who qualify as legitimate change agents. His own work prioritised collective discussion to deliver a shared understanding of what counts as meaningful change and to work through alternative ways forward with complementary interventions that increase the chances of securing outcomes that are positive, and recognised as such on a consensual basis (Lewin, 1947). Lewin's personal ethical stance and commitment to participative management as an effective means of achieving social as well as performance-related changes in the way organisations function is consistent with the prevailing logic of empowering, enabling and inclusive innovation in IDS. It also jars with the over-rationalised, exclusive and conservative functionalism that is the staple diet of OCM.

There is now a greater appreciation of the distortive tendency in prescriptive accounts of Lewin's scholarship, and more obvious critical reaction to oversimplification, to the purging of ethical content and the tendency to boil it all down to 'technician thinking' (Collins, 1998). More sensitive reviews of this foundational figure in the field of change management encourage alternative, collective ways of setting the aims and means of achieving change (Cummings et al., 2016; Burnes et al., 2018). OCM is deeply entrenched, however, and does little to encourage critical reflection about the respective contributions of managerial and other potential change agents. The core assumptions continue to favour managerial hierarchies as the source of objective expertise rather than irrational resistance, attributing reticence and obstructionism almost exclusively to other professionals and employees.

Heroic Change Management

Prescriptive approaches frequently assert that effective change initiatives are driven from the top of organisational hierarchies, by exceptional leaders and enlightened managers who can be relied upon to articulate a clear vision, translate this into operational requirement, and then cascade related targets and alterations down through hierarchies to elicit commitment by means of appropriate motivational techniques. The prescriptive mantra is that executive insight and authority is necessary to lead change efforts and ensure that members of staff are receptive and properly prepared to execute the approved strategy. Change champions are credited with driving the process via careful planning and decisive action (Kotter, 1996; Varkey and Antonio, 2010).

Much of this is focused on overcoming barriers to change, tackling resistance and leading employees to an eventual acceptance of managerial wisdom. A great deal of attention is given to classifying reasons for resistance and explaining why particular categories of worker fail to grasp or seek to challenge management decisions (Martin, 2001; NHS National Institute for Health and Clinical Excellence, 2007). A recurring theme is that staff are likely to resist rational change strategies and therefore have a propensity towards irrational and self-seeking behaviour that change agents must be ready to overcome. OCM overlaps with accounts of transformative leadership in this respect, sharing a preoccupation with the transformation of subordinates rather than managerial standards and practices (Burnes et al., 2018).

In IDS, clinicians are frequently identified as the most powerful sources of resistance, much of it in the misguided category of inherently conservative and narrowly collegiate, driven by an allegiance to professional societies and standards which threaten the prudent management of resources (Callaly and Arya, 2005). Fears about the erosion of medical power are presented as taking precedence over financial accountability, fostering restrictive practices and destabilising producer interests that can stymie rational change initiatives (Doolin, 2003). Faced with this degree of difficulty, the prescriptive literature presents managerial change agency as a heroic struggle to enact necessary change or, more specifically, a seemingly objective OCM view of what this entails. The default position is acting on or against non-managerial stakeholders, rather than with them, to make people more susceptible to the objective insight and approach of the rational change agent.

There is evidence of growing unease with this privileging of managerial authority and with the tendency in OCM to approach a bunker mentality against other perspectives from questionable assumptions about good change and rational practice. Alternative interpretations are too easily neglected or dismissed, while senior managerial insights and capabilities are exaggerated. As others have noted, the readiness to contrast rational management with irrational resistance suggests that OCM is infused by a worrying intolerance and essential authoritarianism that is fundamentally problematic (Boudon, 1986; Burnes et al., 2018).

The conventional wisdom behind top-down leaderism and managerialism was seriously tested through the Great Recession of 2007/8 and found wanting as the fallout from executive myopia and excess was exposed in dramatic fashion. The problems that can follow from an over-reliance on top-driven change strategies and unchecked managerialism have also been very clearly revealed in healthcare, through the hospital scandals identified earlier and the recurring crises with resourcing, staffing and service delivery within and beyond the British National Health Service (NHS). Many researchers and commentators are troubled by the actions of formal leaders and senior managers, and equally by the failure to acknowledge and address the fallout from their behaviour in the prescriptive managerial literature (King's Fund, 2011).

Again, this cuts against the grain of so much classic and contemporary scholarship, including Lewin's attention to the counterbalancing influence of reflective learning and the participative management of change. These are in deficit as far as OCM is concerned. For all the attention that it gives to change and to dysfunctional and misguided reactions, there has been no obvious reappraisal of managerialism in this movement as a result of the various scandals. The faith that prescriptive commentators invest in the orthodoxy seems undiminished, as if resistant in itself to change. This is not a new assessment, although it merits wider recognition:

> In reimagining organisational change leadership, it is ironic how resistant to change the status quo has been. Once again, Calas and Smircich (1991: 568) were ahead of us when suggesting that for leadership '…the more things change, the more they remain the same'.

(Burnes et al., 2018: 14)

Empirical evidence confirms that change initiatives are frequently imposed on a top-down basis without a developed sense of the role and contribution of non-managerial participants. Writing about experiences in the education sector, Grant (2009: 20) concludes that 'for all the talk of stakeholder participation and engagement, change management has been a one-way street of authoritarianism'. Similar reactions are evident in healthcare, with regular references to managerial imposition, curtailed empowerment and tokenistic inclusion (Doolin, 2003; Callaly and Arya, 2005). Clinicians are often on the receiving end of top-driven change that aims to reshape professional practice and conditions of service, with little or no formal scope to exert a constructive independent influence.

In a detailed study of change management in a New Zealand hospital, Doolin (2003) discovered variations in calculated managerialism, with direct and also more subtle attempts to curtail the behaviour of clinicians. These were informed by familiar ambitions to promote a more business-like responsibility with resources. Initial efforts to impose management controls and cut treatment costs were replaced by attempts to instil managerial values and encourage clinicians to regulate their own performance as 'clinician managers'. The OCM notion of empowerment is evident in this, with hospital managers claiming that responsibility for efficiency was moving closer to patients. However, this was a matter of holding clinicians accountable for the costs arising from their decisions about treatment. The emphasis was firmly placed on applying management, acting on clinicians to ensure greater compliance with established managerial priorities. This was top-driven change, with managers anticipating that clinicians would internalise cost concerns and exhibit more disciplined behaviour. This was not about giving them an independent voice in management decision-making, or ensuring the managers were more responsive to front line clinical concerns.

Medical reactions were highly critical and largely resistant, with many arguing that this one-way managerial change initiative was out of step with their professional obligation to provide the best care for patients. There were signs of anxiety and disillusionment as traditional values of caring and cooperation seemed to clash with a managerialist discourse about financial restrictions and direct accountability for the use of resources. In this regard, Doolin's account is indicative of wider academic research on the impact and unintended consequences of OCM interventions (Collins, 1998; Cooke, 2006). There is no shortage of evidence that imposed, top-driven change programmes leave people feeling disengaged, considering themselves to be objects or victims of change (Davidson, 2015). This can produce disaffection, low morale, a lack of responsiveness, problems with absenteeism and recruitment difficulties that have a major bearing upon service. The OCM response is often that the process has been misunderstood and needs to be more clearly explained, or worse, that such reactions are unreasonable or unduly negative and need to be overcome by determined management action.

In a discussion of change leadership in healthcare, Ward (2017) recognises that preoccupations with resistance and negativity often reveal more about the orientations of prescriptive writers than the shortcomings of those affected by change projects. There is a frequent imbalance in evaluations of change initiatives, with critical and unfavourable responses judged from the standpoint of frustrated change agents (Ford et al., 2008). Academic accounts that give credence to other voices demonstrate that members of staff are usually acutely aware of the nature and consequences of change, and are not reliant on managerial explanations for a more informed or realistic understanding of what is happening to them. Nor are they inherently resistant or reluctant to change. Indeed, their attitude can be more open and welcoming than orthodox commentators imagine, although their sense of necessary and desirable change can be very different.

What professional and wider employee groups question or resist may have less to do with change *per se* than the way it is imposed or influenced by the prescriptive orthodoxy (Paton and McCalman, 2000; Callaly and Arya, 2005). When considered from the standpoint of front line staff, managerial orientations and interventions can look altogether more disabling than useful, ill-considered rather than informed, heavy-handed instead of supportive or appreciative. The insularity and traditionalism of managerial grades can seem to be at odds with local insights and understandings that have the potential to inform change processes, yet are neglected or dismissed as a matter of reflex, from a naïve faith in the primacy of managerial roles and reinforcing logic of OCM.

There is some evidence of realist workers intervening to compensate for this, introducing organisational changes on an informal group basis, despite management processes (Fincham, 1989; Beirne, 2008). This reveals that non-managerial staff form their own views about change and act on them, often constructively, collectively and to significant effect. Hence, their involvement needs to be taken seriously in change management, as a matter of principle, though also as a source of independent influence that will have a bearing on outcomes in some way or another.

The practical implications of scholarship on this front are often underdeveloped. It demonstrates that change management is not just the province of senior managers, however, that the impetus for change can come from many levels in work organisations. Lessons can be drawn from this to disrupt unitary thinking and push back against the restrictive legacy of OCM so that knowledgeable stakeholders – from employee, professional and management groups – can find an authentic voice in change processes.

Principled Management for a Principle-Driven Service

While pursuing the Democratic Party nomination for President of the United States, and subsequently campaigning for this office, Barak Obama enthused people with the slogan, 'Change We Can Believe In' (Obama, 2008). This phrase captured the mood of the time, underlining the importance of inclusion and effective representation while magnifying the popular perception that meaningful change connects with the full range of interests, experiences and interpretations across a community. In light of expressed concerns for inclusion and empowerment in IDS, it also provides a powerful rallying call for more grounded, consistent and progressive approaches to achieving change than OCM can deliver.

An alternative change agency can be rooted, quite reasonably and safely, in organisational insights and self-transforming capacities that cut across occupational and professional boundaries. This contention is supported by a strong tradition of applied scholarship that draws managerial knowledge from non-managerial groups. Pioneering examples in the British coal industry called attention to the viability of distributed change agency, with influential figures at the Tavistock Institute of Human Relations recognising, supporting and developing voluntary employee innovations in working practice that counteracted damaging elements of imposed change programmes. Theorist-practitioners such as Trist (1963) tapped into the local knowledge and self-adjusting activism of miners, underlining the importance of what Fincham (1989) calls 'natural workgroups'. These are creative combinations of front line employees who act on local insights and tacit abilities, often spontaneously, to make their own improvements.

Subsequent critical writing has argued for a reframing of change management as a grounded and collaborative process that harnesses the 'natural workgroup' propensities of employees, though with direct channels of independent influence and decision-making authority to prevent these being diluted or undermined by an expert rationale or recurring managerialism (Beirne, 2008). There are calls for more applied research to nurture and sustain this alternative approach, recognising that it sits uneasily with traditional ways of thinking and managing, which have also derailed or curtailed employee participation schemes in the past (Beirne, 2017a). Progress is considered to be an uphill struggle, requiring persistence and creativity to address negative reactions and to negotiate barriers that currently inhibit distributed decision-making. Demonstrating that grassroots perspectives contribute to a rounded understanding of change and produce more promising interventions than OCM will not be enough in itself. This sense of cautious realism and these arguments apply with just as much force to healthcare as any other area of collaborative work.

Several commentators have pointed to the significance of 'natural workgroup' tendencies and distributed change agency among clinicians, at least in initiating improvements. From detailed case research, Buchanan et al. (2007) show that meaningful change can be introduced in the absence of rational management planning and direction, when 'nobody is in charge'. The focus of their attention is cancer care services in a British hospital, where specialist nurses and doctors established an agenda for change incrementally and informally, enlisting other contributions from colleagues and managers as the collective understanding of what was possible and useful evolved. A core group was identified at the centre of this, stimulating discussion about weaknesses and ways forward for prostate cancer care, and then both applying initiative and eliciting it from others in a wider 'natural workgroup' of informal change agents.

The researchers acknowledge that in this instance the hospital context was conducive to the distributed approach. The priority attached to cancer services, a lack of stability with executive level appointments and a reluctance to direct change from above created space for the front line professionals 'to get on with it'. Buchanan et al. (2007) also recognise that the 'nobody in charge' theme may unsettle traditionalists and be dismissed as an accident or the product of exceptional circumstances. Distributed change agency is not an isolated or unusual occurrence in healthcare, however (Beirne, 2017a). Another telling example was presented at a leadership conference in Dublin, this time with advanced nurse practitioners facilitating grassroots collaboration across two Irish hospitals to provide more equitable care for patients arriving with chest pains (O'Toole, 2016). A nurse-led consultation service was established from this to support patients suspected of coronary heart disease. In line with the previous case, this initiative emerged from local insights, relying upon the *de facto* leadership abilities of clinical staff who did not regard themselves as leaders yet recognised weaknesses and mobilised with others to make significant changes. They also devised an assessment methodology to demonstrate the relative success of their innovation, attracting subsequent recognition and formal support for their approach.

Clearly, successful change in healthcare is not a matter for professional managers alone. It benefits from everyday leadership insights and managerial interventions that are cultivated collaboratively in 'natural workgroups'. Making more of this capacity through enabling arrangements, supportive policies, development opportunities and dissemination programmes for collective learning seems sensible and also consistent with the emphasis now given to respect, inclusion and empowerment. It will be challenging, nonetheless. The legacy of orthodox thinking in management circles and the memory of its application among clinical and other front line staff will be difficult to counteract.

Managers will be nervous about bringing natural workgroups to the fore. Some will feel that their personal authority is undermined by distributed change agency. Members of staff may believe that they are straying over boundaries that are rigid and non-negotiable, and feel hesitant or vulnerable. Others will be cautious or reticent on the grounds that their informal group processes insulated them, compensating for the unpalatable consequences of directive management, and that these are being appropriated, cynically incorporated into the organisational mainstream or subjected to a traditional logic of control.

Research evidence points to the potency and longevity of such views and the importance of circumspect care and ethical pragmatism when attempting to reconstitute management as a genuinely participative process (Alvesson and Spicer, 2012). New management development programmes will be needed if distributed change agency is to be embedded in health organisations as routine practice. Realistically, these will need to challenge and support in equal measure, stimulating reflective capabilities among practitioners so that managers are more responsive to local insights and clinicians can believe that change management is an important part of their role.

Ensuring that those in formal management positions are less susceptible to OCM and better equipped to play a constructive part in sustaining a distributed approach will certainly involve a 'back to basics' reappraisal of what their own contribution entails. Insights gleaned from the applied work of Trist, Lewin and the other participative management enthusiasts identified in this chapter can help with this. Accounts of how they allied themselves with natural workgroups and tapped into repertoires of employee knowledge and active change agency provide invaluable pointers to complementary managerial capabilities and techniques. They also counteract any anxiety about the diminution of management, demonstrating that positional authority is still necessary, on occasion, to promote progressive change, to channel grassroots resistance against debilitating management practices and claim space for reforming initiatives to take hold. This is evident with alternative sources of management learning, from the civil rights and feminist movements, for example, which are neglected in business school education, yet complement developmental programmes in participative management. To paraphrase a comment by Alvesson and Spicer (2012: 385), positional authority is compatible with distributed change agency, although it is important only part of the time, on certain issues, and for enabling rather than curtailing responsible autonomy and shared decision-making.

Extending the appetite for *de facto* change management among clinicians and front line staff will depend upon the environment in which they operate and the extent to which they feel comfortable engaging in 'natural workgroup' innovations and confident about challenging managerialism. Many psychiatrists and doctors share an antipathy towards management, though also a conservative attachment to professional standing and medical hierarchies (Beirne, 2017a). Progress towards distributed change agency will not be well served if one set of sectional interests are substituted for another, however. Once again, the principled, inclusive and empowering approach of Lewin and Trist is instructive. If change agency is to be redistributed from the top of authority structures, sectional claims on influence and expertise must give way to collective and complementary contributions across established clinical and professional boundaries. Lewin and Trist developed their practice from an appreciation of the insights and innovative potential throughout workplace communities, with an ethical commitment to support mutual learning and joint decision-making for the widest benefit. Issues of culture and gender have a bearing upon this approach and can be anticipated in healthcare where nursing and medical contributions to collaborative care teams often reflect the working out of historical stereotypes and inequalities (Beirne, 2017b). Development programmes that aim to draw greater benefits from the distributed change agency of clinicians will need to be sensitive to attitudes and understandings that might limit cohesion and inhibit 'natural workgroup' tendencies. Addressing expectations and tensions relating to professional standing and interaction may be even more important for clinical engagement in change management than tackling negative perceptions about straying into 'lesser' managerial roles.

Conclusion

Grappling with change is nothing new in healthcare, although current attempts are complicated by the legacy of earlier efforts and preoccupations. Change management is now a major field of study and practice, yet these two realms are frequently disconnected, making it difficult for health professionals (be they in managerial, clinical or support roles) to disentangle themselves from the restrictions of prescriptive orthodoxy and sustain alternative means of achieving change collaboratively.

The principles of inclusion and empowerment that are now openly endorsed by policy makers and IDS authorities are not self-evidently consistent with the rationalism, managerialism and leaderism that permeates the traditional repertoire of change management, even if the vocabulary occasionally seems to overlap. The meaning attached to these terms by management writers and consultants regularly falls short of reasonable expectations about levels of mutual learning, sharing and joint decision-making. Indeed, value-based understandings are usually out of focus, as technician thinking predominates and empowerment is reduced to an instrumental means by which senior figures try to elicit information and commitment from staff.

Consistency is important for principled professions and service organisations and should link strategic intentions with developments in the conduct of work and management, certainly if the contributions of front line staff are to be sustained for service improvement. When expressed priorities and public statements are out of line with the everyday experiences of managed staff, evidence suggests that problems with the recruitment and retention of talented people often follow, along with growing distrust and slipping standards. The well-publicised priorities for changing IDS must be evident 'on the ground'.

Distributed change agency provides a viable way of aligning declared principles with innovative practice and the capacity for improving and reforming that is evident in natural workgroups. There is more to be gained from understanding how this can be extended and solidified as a regular feature of organisational performance than from attempting to master conventional change management methods.

Key Concepts Discussed

- Controllability, leaderism and managerialism in prescriptive literature.
- The growing pluralism of concepts, interpretations and alternative options for understanding and managing change.
- Competing conceptualisations of empowering, enabling and supportive management.
- Consistency in the articulation and operationalisation of expressed principles and organisational priorities across IDS levels, roles and responsibilities.
- The logic of grounding and decentralising change processes, recognising 'natural work groups' and tapping into repertoires of established local knowledge and expertise.

Influential Reports and Policy Documents

■ Department of Health. 2012. *Transforming Care: A National Response to Winterbourne View Hospital.* London: HMSO.
Transforming Care and Commissioning Steering Group Report. 2014. *Winterbourne View: Time for Change.* NHS England. Available at: https://www.england.nhs.uk/wp-content/uploads/2014/11/transforming-commissioning-serv ices.pdf.
   – Official reports setting out the lessons to be drawn from IDS care failures and establishing the terms for fresh policy and debates about future priorities and organisational changes.
■ O'Mahony, C. 2014. *What Happened in Bungalow 3: How the Law Must Change.* Dublin: RTE Prime Time.
BBC. 2012. *The Hospital That Stopped Caring.* London: BBC Panorama.
   – Landmark reports by investigative journalists that still provide an impetus for change and improvement in IDS.
■ UK Strengthening the Commitment Steering Group. 2015. *Strengthening the Commitment: Living the Commitment.* Edinburgh: The Scottish Government.
   – An example of growing concerns to expand the job roles of IDS staff and establish clearer insights into the significance of frontline leadership contributions to improvement processes.

Examples of Prescriptive and Managerial Approaches

■ Callaly, T., and D. Arya. 2005. Organizational Change Management in Mental Health. *Australasian Psychiatry 13*: 120–123.
■ Davidson, J. 2015. What's All the Buzz about Change Management? *Healthcare Management Forum 28*: 118–120.

■ Forthman, A., Wooster, L.D., Hill, W., Homa-Lowry, J. and S. DesHarnais. 2003. Insights into Successful Change Management: Empirically Supported Techniques for Improving Medical Practice Patterns. *American Journal of Medical Quality 18*: 181–189.
■ Kotter, J. 1996. *Leading Change*. Boston, MA: Harvard Business School Press.
■ Varkey, P., and K. Antonio. 2010. Change Management for Effective Quality Improvements: A Primer. *American Journal of Medical Quality 25*: 268–273.

Critical, Corrective and Alternative Literature on Change Management

■ Collins, D. 1998. *Organizational Change: Sociological Perspectives*. London: Routledge.
  - This book provides an excellent antidote to the lingering attraction of prescriptive models and the ongoing influence of populist management gurus. It debunks orthodox preoccupations, assumptions and assertions with clarity and precision, at the same time casting light on why they appeal to practitioners.
■ Cummings, S., Bridgeman, T., and K. Brown. 2016. Unfreezing Change as Three Steps: Rethinking Kurt Lewin's Legacy for Change Management. *Human Relations 69*: 33–60.
  - This paper challenges oversimplified accounts of Lewin's scholarly contribution and influence on management practice, offering a counter-history of change theory.
■ Sturdy, A., and C. Grey. 2003. Beneath and Beyond Organizational Change Management: Exploring Alternatives. *Organization 10*: 651–662.
  - This article introduces a special edition of the influential journal *Organization* which explores alternative perspectives on organisational change management.

Useful Websites

- ACAS, The British Advisory, Conciliation and Arbitration Service http://www.acas.org.uk/index.aspx?articleid=4669 Glasgow School of Art, Cultures of Innovation Collaborative Ventures www.gsa.ac.uk/research/design-innovation/creating-cultures-of-innovation/
  - Examples of more grounded and participative approaches to change managements.
- The Katzenbach Centre, PwC and 'Strategy and' business consulting community https://www.strategy-business.com/article/00255?gko=9d35b; https://www.strategyand.pwc.co m/katzenbach-center; https://www.strategy-business.com/article/m00024
  - These sites exemplify the logic of approach and prescriptive interventions promoted by commercial consultants and the management solutions industry.

References

Alvesson, T., and A. Spicer. 2012. Critical Leadership Studies: The Case for Critical Performativity. *Human Relations 65*: 367–390.
BBC. 2012. *The Hospital That Stopped Caring.* London: BBC Panorama.
Beirne, M. 2008. Idealism and the Applied Relevance of Research on Employee Participation. *Work, Employment and Society 22*: 675–693.
Beirne, M. 2017a. The Reforming Appeal of Distributed Leadership: Recognizing Concerns and Contradictory Tendencies. *British Journal of Healthcare Management 23*: 262–270.
Beirne, M. 2017b. Leadership, Gender and Equality: Challenging Terms for Post-Heroic Theory and Practice? In E. Curtis and J. Cullen (Eds.) *Leadership and Change for the Health Professional.* London: Open University Press. pp. 81–96.
Boudon, R. 1986. *Theories of Social Change.* Cambridge: Polity Press.

Buchanan, D., Addicott, R., Fitzgerald, L., Ferlie, E. and J. Baeza. 2007. Nobody in Charge: Distributed Change Agency in Healthcare. *Human Relations 60*: 1065–1090.

Burnes, B. 2004. Kurt Lewin and the Planned Approach to Change: A Re-appraisal. *Journal of Management Studies 41*: 977–1002.

Burnes, B., Hughes, M., and T. By. 2018. Reimagining Organisational Change Leadership. *Leadership* 14: 141–158 .

Calas, M., and L. Smircich. 1991. Voicing Seduction to Silence Leadership. *Organization Studies 12*: 567–602.

Callaly, T., and D. Arya. 2005. Organizational Change Management in Mental Health. *Australasian Psychiatry 13*: 120–123.

Collins, D. 1998. *Organizational Change: Sociological Perspectives.* London: Routledge.

Cooke, H. 2006. Seagull Management and the Control of Nursing Work. *Work, Employment and Society 20*: 223–243.

Cummings, S., Bridgeman, T. and K. Brown. 2016. Unfreezing Change as Three Steps: Rethinking Kurt Lewin's Legacy for Change Management. *Human Relations 69*(1): 33–60.

Davidson, J. 2015. What's All the Buzz about Change Management? *Healthcare Management Forum 28*: 118–120.

Department of Health. 2001. *Valuing People: A New Strategy for Learning Disability for the 21st Century.* London: HMSO [Cm 5086].

Doolin, B. 2003. Narratives of Change: Discourse, technology and Organization. *Organization 10*: 751–770.

Fincham, R. 1989. Natural Workgroups and the Process of Job Design. *Employee Relations 11*: 17–22.

Ford, J., Ford, L. and A. D'Amelio. 2008. Resistance to Change: The Rest of the Story. *Academy of Management Review 33*: 362–377.

Francis, R. 2013. *Report of the Mid Staffordshire NHS Foundation Trust Public Inquiry: Executive Summary.* London: HMSO.

Grant, N. 2009. Schools of Little Thought: Why Change Management Hasn't Worked. *Improving Schools 12*: 19–32.

Keogh, B. 2013. *Review into the Quality of Care and Treatment Provided by 14 Hospital Trusts in England: Overview Report.* London: HMSO.

King's Fund. 2011. *The Future of Leadership and Management in the NHS: No More Heroes.* London: The King's Fund.

Kotter, J. 1996. *Leading Change.* Boston, MA: Harvard Business School Press.

Levasseur, R. 2001. People Skills: Change Management Tools: Lewin's Change Model. *Interfaces 31*: 71–73.

Lewin, K. 1947. Frontiers in Group Dynamics: Concept, Method and Reality in Social Science; Equilibria and Social Change. *Human Relations 1*: 5–41.

Martin, J. 2001. *Organisational Behaviour.* London: Thompson Learning.

NHS National Institute for Health and Clinical Excellence. 2007. *How to Change Practice.* London: NIHCE.

Obama, B. 2008. *Change We Can Believe In: Barack Obama's Plan to Renew America's Promise.* New York, NY: Random House.

O'Mahony, C. 2014. *What Happened in Bungalow 3: How the Law Must Change.* Dublin: RTE Prime Time.

O'Reilly, D. and M. Reed. 2010. 'Leaderism': An Evolution of Managerialism in UK Public Service Reforms. *Public Administration 88*: 960–978.

O'Toole, J. 2016. Connecting Cardiology Services through Advanced Nursing Practice within the Dublin Midlands Hospital Group in Ireland. *Inaugural Conference on Healthcare Leadership.* Dublin: Trinity College 21 June.

Paton, R. and J. McCalman. 2000. *Change Management: A Guide to Effective Implementation.* London: Sage.

Sturdy, A. and C. Grey. 2003. Beneath and Beyond Organizational Change Management: Exploring Alternatives. *Organization 10*: 651–662.

Transforming Care and Commissioning Steering Group Report. 2014. *Winterbourne View: Time for Change.* London: NHS England.

Trist, E. 1963. *Organisational Choice.* London: Tavistock.

UK Strengthening the Commitment Steering Group. 2015. *Strengthening the Commitment: Living the Commitment.* Edinburgh: The Scottish Government.

Varkey, P. and K. Antonio. 2010. Change Management for Effective Quality Improvements: A Primer. *American Journal of Medical Quality 25*: 268–273.

Ward, M. 2017. Leading Change in Healthcare. In E. Curtis and J. Cullen (Eds.) *Leadership and Change for the Health Professional.* London: Open University Press. pp. 193–208.

Chapter 7

Achieving Change Through Grassroots Education and Leadership

Maria Paiewonsky and Debra Hart

Contents

Chapter Topics

- **Background of postsecondary education for students who experience intellectual disability in the United States.**
- **National overview of postsecondary education for students who experience intellectual disability.**
- **One state's efforts to grow the option of going to college for students who experience intellectual disability.**
- **How family and student experiences should be used to shape policy.**
- **Promoting family and student involvement with state-level partners.**

Introduction

Creating a national movement that embraces inclusive higher education for students who experience intellectual disability requires consideration of multiple factors and stakeholders. First, it is necessary to understand the historical context of such a movement. Then it is important to examine the key areas that are impacted. These include restructuring personnel preparation programs to align with inclusive postsecondary education expectations and practices; collaborating with special education administrators to create effective and responsive policies and practices; providing in-service professional development for college faculty that emphasizes universally designed instruction, engagement, and assessment; and meeting with college administration, whose leadership can solidify a mission of inclusiveness and belonging in higher education.

Building a culture of inclusive higher education also involves collaboration with policymakers at every level of government that influences higher education participation, including local, state, regional, and federal policy leaders. At the heart of collaboration are the contributions of parents and students, whose advocacy and peer-to-peer networking can compel leadership to effect change.

Historical Context

The United States had a scant number of higher education programs that supported students with intellectual disability in higher education for some 25 to 30 years. These programs operated in silos and were typically focused on independent living or life skills and/or employment readiness. A common theme across programs was their segregated approach to service delivery and their varying degrees of connection to their larger host institute of higher education.

Overall, there were few higher education options, no legislation, no research or data, no knowledge base or little to no understanding of the existing programs, and low-to-no demand for such higher education programs for students who experience intellectual disability.

From the late 1990s until 2007, change began to slowly transpire, as there was a slight increase in federal and state funding and therefore an increase in the number of post-secondary education programs that created access to higher education for students who experience intellectual disability. This activity established baseline awareness of and profiles on postsecondary education programs (PSE) for students who experience intellectual disability, contained in the first national PSE program database (Think College, 2003). This activity also served to increase knowledge of and demand for more PSE initiatives for students who experience intellectual disability.

By 2007, there was considerable growth in understanding of the variance between PSE programs due to an increase in Federal and state funding. In 2008, the Higher Education Opportunities Act (HEOA) was passed. The HEOA created groundbreaking opportunities for the growth of and guidance in the development of PSE initiatives for students who experience intellectual disability.

The legislation also created a comprehensive federal program around inclusive PSE. This program included some key features such as model demonstration projects, a national coordinating center, Comprehensive Transition Programs where students who experience intellectual disability are eligible for Federal financial aid, a standard definition of intellectual disability, and key components of a PSE program (e.g., academic, social, independent living, and employment).

The Story of One State's Efforts to Make the Choice of Going to College a Reality for Students Who Experience Intellectual Disability: Capitalizing on Distributive Leadership

The inclusion of HEOA guidance to include students who experience intellectual disability in higher education was based, in part, on success that was achieved in Massachusetts where advocates, researchers, and families created inclusive dual enrollment opportunities for students who experience intellectual disability beginning in 2007. Resulting from their nine years of work, Massachusetts became the first United States state to secure legislative support and funding to develop a statewide network of inclusive dual or concurrent enrollment initiatives for students who experience intellectual disability who were between the ages of 18 and 22 and who were still enrolled in high school.

This was possible, in large part, because key stakeholders representing research, legislative advocacy, and public policy collaborated to form a comprehensive strategy of advocacy. By adopting a model of distributive leadership (Bierly et al., 2016; Harris, 2014), stakeholders fanned out across the state, tapping needed leadership by expertise. This included mobilizing state legislators who in turn reached out to their constituents to garner support, parent advocates who used their formal and informal networks to build parent and student awareness, and disability advocates who reached out to teacher and faculty practitioners who could testify about their own positive experiences with inclusive higher education practices. Advocates also turned to students who experience intellectual disability themselves to publicly describe their experiences, before and after having a college opportunity.

This distributive approach to leadership and system change has contributed to an emerging model of inclusive secondary and postsecondary education transition services in Massachusetts. As a result, there is expanding awareness of and innovation for inclusive higher education across the state.

To understand the need for these opportunities, it is helpful to grasp the context of education for transition-aged students with disabilities in Massachusetts. There are nearly 8,000 students with low-incidence disabilities (e.g., intellectual disability, multiple disabilities, autism, developmental disability) between the ages of 14 to 22 in the state, and approximately 3,787 of those students are between the ages of 18 to 22. Of these nearly 4,000 students, 3,027 are classified as having "high needs" to achieve school success and only 6% have access to full or partially inclusive education. The remaining 94% are in substantially separate classrooms or separate private/public day and residential schools (MA DESE, 2015).

Numerous efforts have been made to address the staggering percentage of students who are likely being tracked into separate education settings. Two initiatives in particular, the Massachusetts Inclusive Concurrent Enrollment Initiative and An Act to promote the successful transition of students with disabilities to postsecondary education, employment, and independent living, known as the Transition Bill, stand out as having a positive influence on transition and postsecondary education participation for students who experience intellectual disability in the state, with much credit going to the collaborative leadership among key stakeholders (Massachusetts Legislature, 2011, 2012).

Collaboration with Legislative Advocates and Policymakers

At the Institute for Community Inclusion at the University of Massachusetts Boston, staff had used state grants and federal model demonstration grant funds from the late 1990s through the early-to-mid 2000s to pilot and then expand inclusive postsecondary education opportunities for students who experience intellectual disability, aged 18 to 22 years old, whose only post-school option until then was receiving sub-separate education that focused on life skills and pre-work activities at facility-based sheltered workshops (Hart et al., 2001). There was no option to extend formal education beyond high school, and few options to obtain real paid work.

At the start of this initiative, staff partnered with a local school district and a neighboring two-year community college in five communities across the state to provide students with a model of transition planning. This model included person-centered planning to identify student strengths and job preferences, access to inclusive college classes, support to engage in campus life beyond the classroom with college peers, and integrated, community-based work. The model also included establishing a collaborative interagency team (Student

Support Team) to develop individual services and supports for students who expressed an interest in postsecondary education (Hart et al., 2001).

After seven years of piloting this work, this promising model of transition services was brought to the attention of disability advocates at Massachusetts Advocates for Children (MAC), who had a long, successful record of working with state legislators to overhaul education policies for students with disabilities. Their skills at legislative advocacy and ongoing communications with key policy stakeholders led to state approval of legislative funds to expand inclusive higher education opportunities across the state, beginning in 2006.

With the expertise of MAC to facilitate discussions regarding complicated policy issues between the state local education agency and the state's department of higher education, a request for proposals was issued by the end of the year, making way for eight new state-funded pilot programs called the Massachusetts Inclusive Concurrent Enrollment initiative (MAICEI) to support students across the state (MA DESE, 2009). Since that time, the state has supported another six college-school partnerships, bringing the total to 13, and supporting over 800 students who experience intellectual disability to attend college as part of their transition services (MA EOE, 2016). Outreach to legislative advocates and policymakers allowed a greater number of students with intellectual disability to access higher education in Massachusetts, whether or not their district was engaged in a grant initiative.

Forming an Interagency Taskforce

To prepare for MAICEI, an interagency taskforce was organized between the MA Department of Elementary and Secondary Education, the Department of Higher Education, and other adult state service agencies and advocates to work out a mission for this unprecedented collaboration, and also the practical details for providing an inclusive dual enrollment experience for students who experience intellectual disability (Massachusetts House and Senate Co-Chairs of the Joint Committee on Higher Education, 2014). This was no small undertaking, but given the advocacy already achieved, bringing on college administrators was viewed as including another layer of experts, distributing and expanding leadership to another group of stakeholders. This interagency team, including college administrators, tackled many policies that would stand as barriers to college participation unless they worked it out at the state level.

In regard to higher education policies, the group made decisions about how "ability to benefit" practices such as placement tests would be waived for students eligible for inclusive dual enrollment, that audit policies which allow students to access courses as non-matriculating students would be aligned across the campuses, and that colleges could waive prerequisite requirements for courses that otherwise would be unavailable to students.

On the secondary education side, the group addressed policies that allowed students to receive transition services, which include college access away from high school. They provided guidance to school administrators to adjust attendance policies so that students did not have to physically start their day at the high school to be marked present. They also advised school administrators on how to work out policies, often with their union representatives, to adjust staff schedules so that students who needed support from the school could follow a typical college schedule rather than a school schedule. This included attending classes during school vacations and taking the spring break week off.

With these policies developed, the taskforce then developed the criteria for a request for proposals (RFP) from college-school partnerships across the state to develop a program of inclusive dual enrollment services. Since 2007, the MAICEI partnerships have grown from eight to thirteen, giving 100 to

120 students each year the opportunity to include college in their transition services (Executive Office of Education, 2017).

Meeting with College Campus Leaders

For some college campus leaders, running inclusive dual enrollment initiatives on campus can initially seem like an incongruous idea. Aligning inclusive postsecondary education with other college priorities, such as student enrollment and retention, coping with rising costs that lead to increased tuition, and faculty and program development can often seem like a formidable undertaking for college administrators.

In discussing inclusive postsecondary education with college presidents and other administrators, advocates learned from their Department of Higher Education (DHE) partners that aligning these efforts with the mission of the college, particularly mission statements that emphasized serving the community and embracing a diverse student body, was important. They also learned that at the practical level, communicating with college presidents at their quarterly Board of Higher Education meetings would give them the best chance to advocate for inclusive postsecondary education and to communicate the benefits of opening their colleges to students who experience intellectual disability.

Advocates, sponsored by their DHE partners, presented at multiple meetings and also invited two college students who experience intellectual disability to share their experiences about attending college. Presenting at these meetings gave advocates and students the opportunity to highlight for college presidents that students who experience intellectual disability, just like their peers without disabilities, are interested in accessing college for a variety of reasons: to pursue career goals, to continue their education, to follow their peers, to meet family expectations, and to prepare for post-school life.

Communicating with College Departments

In addition to communications at the state level, college coordinators who were interested in launching dual enrollment initiatives on their campuses were provided with ongoing support to effectively communicate this initiative, using formal and informal methods to reach out to college faculty, professional staff, and campus departments (Paiewonsky et al., 2015). When college-school partnerships were awarded funds through the RFP process to create inclusive dual enrollment programs, leadership for this initiative was expanded, this time at the individual campus level. Each initiative to support MAICEI needs allies on campus, who recognize the important roles in disability services, the registrar's office, and academic advising, not only to prepare students who experience intellectual disability for college, but to include them as members of a welcoming and diverse college community.

Advocates also emphasized to coordinators that they needed to align with existing college protocols from everything to course registration to college orientation, to emphasize that the model was meant to be fully inclusive, rather than a specialized segregated program with different rules. To establish allies across the campus, college coordinators with some experience recommended that others in this role take advantage of formal department meetings, as well as informal meeting opportunities. In these more informal conversations between coordinators and campus personnel, discussions can be about sharing student success stories and can include more opportunities for questions and clarification (Paiewonsky et al., 2013).

Offering Professional Development to Faculty

The experiences that students have in college courses are central to college access. To prepare faculty who would be supporting students who experience intellectual disability, and for those who expressed an interest, professional development was offered on principles and strategies of universal design for learning (UDL). For instance, a professor may provide a syllabus that allows for some flexibility in how students engage in class (e.g., large or small groups; hybrid format of in-person and online) and in how the students demonstrate what they know (e.g., selecting a final assignment from a choice of three). In this model of teaching and learning, it is understood that college faculty are confronted by the changing population of students in their courses, and are looking to UDL to help them improve learning experiences for all.

Typically, faculty are not trained as teachers, and professional development in this area is often fragmented. Therefore, an effective strategy has been to explain that applying UDL strategies can help meet the needs of all students, and will likely improve teaching experiences (Boyle, 2013; Love et al., 2017).

Multiple strategies were used to provide professional development to faculty. One approach included forming UDL core teams. On these teams, faculty met regularly to redesign their syllabi so that multiple methods were incorporated for students to access information, engage in learning activities, and communicate through assignments what they learned. As a result, a core group of faculty had developed syllabi that would not only engage students who experience intellectual disability, but all students in their classes. Professional development staff also provided individual faculty with ongoing technical assistance.

One of the most effective methods used to engage faculty in including students who experience intellectual disability in courses was again peer-to-peer networking. At several campuses, college coordinators asked for time at end-of-year faculty meetings to invite faculty and students who worked together over the past semester to describe the experience of an inclusive college course. Overwhelmingly, faculty described their initial misgivings, their surprise that students who experience intellectual disability were as engaged as they were in the course, and most importantly, how their own teaching had changed as a result of using new or different strategies without compromising the content. They also frequently reported that other students in the class appreciated the revised teaching strategies that they themselves benefited from.

Coordinators have reported that these faculty testimonies have gone a long way in encouraging previously hesitant faculty to open their courses to students with intellectual disability. In turn, coordinators promote these testimonies when they are preparing to enroll students for the next semester (Paiewonsky et al., 2013).

Collaborating with Secondary Transition Specialists

For schools who are introduced to MAICEI, leadership is sought from special secondary transition specialists who have an important role in reaching out and communicating this new model of transition services. Their leadership and guidance is critical in discussing with classroom teachers a different way of supporting students, away from the school, but with their support to prepare families, promote self-determination and self-advocacy skills, help students adjust to learning with accommodations, as expected in college rather than full modifications, which they are entitled to in K-12 settings.

Transition specialists also provide leadership in individual education program (IEP) meetings, where they can introduce college as an option for pursuing goals, and advise teams to prepare students for this opportunity by developing appropriate annual goals and benchmarks that align with college-based transition services. Special education administrators, who often oversee transition specialists, use their leadership to communicate this model to school principals, school committee members, and school faculty. This work is especially important as the model grows, because it usually results in schools working to realign and reallocate resources to give more students this inclusive model of transition services rather than the traditional model of special education programming at the high school.

Transition specialists provide leadership in preparing students for these new college-based services. These specialists also introduce families to this new inclusive model, hire and train staff to support students as they transition from school-based to college-based transition services, and work with teachers to develop new schedules, supports, and transportation plans for each student.

Two important responsibilities that transition specialists assume are forming a school district interagency team to grow and support this model for system-wide change, and supporting each student to participate in ongoing person-centered planning. This helps make sure that the foundation of the model—individualized and personalized experiences—is at the forefront of this inclusive postsecondary education opportunity (Hart et al., 2001).

Pre-service and In-service Preparation

Pre-service and in-service professional development advocates, frustrated with inadequate transition services that led to dismal post-school outcomes for students with disabilities, pulled together stakeholders from across Massachusetts, including legal advocates, educators, policymakers, family advocates, and students themselves, to publicly call for change. As a result of this grassroots effort, state legislators passed Chapter 51 of the Acts of 2012: An Act to Promote the Successful Transition of Students with Disabilities to Postsecondary Education, Employment, and Independent Living – H.3720 (Transition Bill press release, 2011).

This law acknowledged the importance and need for highly qualified transition specialists with specialized training to support transition-aged students with intellectual disability (14–22 years). It provided the opportunity for licensed special educators, vocational rehabilitation counselors, school counselors, and school social workers to obtain an "education specialist" endorsement in transition services (Commonwealth of Massachusetts, 2012). As one of only six United States states with a similarly documented endorsement for highly trained transition specialists (Plotner and Simonsen, 2018), this is an important step in recognizing and addressing the gaps in up-to-date transition services training.

At the same time that the Transition Bill was passed, the Office of Special Education Programs (OSEP) in the United States Department of Education (US DOE) was providing discretionary funds for competitive grants to support a number of priority initiatives, including personnel preparation programs, that would adequately prepare personnel to serve students with disabilities, including those with intellectual disability (Plotner and Simonsen, 2018). Staff from the Institute for Community Inclusion were awarded one of these grants to develop a course of study for pre-service personnel who would become among the first in the state to earn the new education specialist endorsement in transition.

With approval from the University of Massachusetts Boston, the transition specialist training program has prepared teachers from across the state for the transition specialist endorsement through courses and applied learning to implement policies and evidence-based practices that prepare students for inclusive higher education and paid integrated employment (UMB, 2018). There are over 20 core assignments in the program that scholars are required to complete and that align with evidence-based transition practices (NTACT, 2016) and the national transition specialist standards outlined by the Council for Exceptional Children's Division on Career Development and Transition (Council for Exceptional Children, 2013). The assignments are built around competencies such as understanding the differences between high school and college, promoting self-advocacy skills, engaging students in college and campus-wide activities, the importance of having paid integrated employment before exiting high school, and teaching students to move from modifications to using college academic accommodations.

Parent Engagement and Leadership

The role of parents in developing inclusive postsecondary options and paid integrated employment for students who experience intellectual disability cannot be underestimated. Their expectations and advocacy for relevant, productive transition services that lead to meaningful post-school lives for their sons and daughters is paramount in developing and expanding inclusive postsecondary education options (Dwyre et al., 2010; Martinez et al., 2012; Rossetti et al., 2016; Yarborough et al., 2014).

In inviting parent leadership, advocates solidify the purpose and demand for improved post-school planning and preparation for their children to prepare for post-school independence. In Massachusetts, a partnership with the state's parent information center, the Federation for Children with Special Needs (no date), led to information sharing through their network of family advocacy groups across the state. Through this broad network, families arranged parent-to-parent meetings to discuss transition, integrated paid employment and postsecondary education. Here, parents could hear information about college and employment opportunities, including how college access can differ for individual students, and how their role changes as their sons or daughters move away from special education and into college and work environments.

Given the hope as well as concerns that some parents may have about new inclusive opportunities (Freedman, 2017; Weir, 2013), parent advocates understood their responsibility to fan out across the state to present this new opportunity and invite parents whose children were involved in MAICEI to honestly talk about their initial fears, how those concerns have been addressed, and what parents and students can expect from an inclusive postsecondary education experience that includes a more age-appropriate model of services: campus engagement, using public transportation, and using technology to fade support.

Transition specialists and inclusive higher education coordinators have also focused on helping parents understand the new role and responsibilities that they can assume to support their son or daughter in higher education (Freedman, 2017), and how inclusive dual enrollment promotes increased independence through fading support and using more college resources (Paiewonsky and Roach, 2010).

Empowering Students Who Experience Intellectual Disability with Leadership Skills

The role of students with intellectual disability was essential for success in appealing to state legislators to vote for funding for MAICEI and to establish the Transition Bill. Julia Landau, a Massachusetts Advocates for Children senior project director who also directs the Disability Education Justice Initiative, stated: "Self-advocates have had an extraordinary impact. Legislative leaders have repeatedly told us that their "yes" vote directly resulted from the testimony they heard or meetings they had with the fellows and other self-advocates" (Weber, 2015). Examples of student advocacy for public policy changes include speaking at state house hearings about the lack of support they receive in school to prepare for goals outside of sheltered work (Norton, 2014; Quinn, 2013); holding a 100-foot petition, spanning the length of the hallway from the governor's office to the House chamber with more than 1,000 signatures from supporters pushing for the Transition Bill (Landau, 2011); and personally making appointments to speak to their legislators one-to-one to make the case that doing nothing is not an option (Gordon, 2015; Transition Taskforce, 2014).

In addition to contributing to public policy contributions, Massachusetts's students with intellectual disability have engaged in participatory action research activities to critically evaluate their college experiences (Paiewonsky et al., 2010; Paiewonsky et al., 2017). Using inclusive research methods, students describe the benefits of their transition and college experiences, and also make recommendations for improvements, such as having better preparation for college and having more opportunities for independence without adult shadowing (Paiewonsky, 2010).

Students have been invited to present their own research findings and experiences at national conferences (Hart et al., 2013; Paiewonsky et al., 2017), and to write stories and practice briefs about these experiences (Hooley and Cardoza, 2018; Wetherby and Hanson, 2015) that are then disseminated through the national Think College website.

Many students with intellectual disability are still not aware that college is a choice for them, nor are they prepared for college during their high school years. To address these gaps, some students who have included college in their transition services have been invited to speak directly to their peers about the benefits of going to college, getting paid employment, and to address their peers' concerns. These student advocates have also made recommendations to teachers about ways that they could better prepare students with intellectual disability for college and integrated paid employment (Massachusetts Advocates for Children, 2018).

Conclusion

Much has changed in the world of higher education for students who experience intellectual disability since the passage of the HEOA in 2008, but not enough. Unfortunately, individuals who experience intellectual disability are still the most excluded population from higher education. This pattern of exclusion originates in K-12 educational settings and extends into adult life service systems where low expectations run rampant, leading to the poorest post-school outcomes of all disability groups. These practices and attitudes have not changed enough, but where higher education programs exist that support students who experience intellectual disability in going to college, attitudes and practices are transforming. College students who experience intellectual disability are far exceeding expectations and continue to demonstrate that they are capable of far more than historically expected. This, in turn, exemplifies the need for students who experience intellectual disability, their families, and professionals to dream big regarding all aspects of life. If students who experience intellectual disability can successfully take inclusive college courses (with accommodations and/or supports) then there is no reason that they could not be included in inclusive academic high school classes where they can be better prepared for college expectations rather than being tracked into traditional functional life skills and independent living classes.

Massachusetts is the story of one state's efforts to change this stagnant view of low expectations and outcomes for students who experience intellectual disability. The state legislature, as a result of grassroots advocacy, came to recognize the need for leadership in K-12 education, higher education, and adult services by supporting a statewide effort to grow higher education opportunities for students who experience intellectual disability. Additionally, Massachusetts identified the need for highly qualified professionals to support this new college-based transition initiative and hence passed the Transition Bill that supports professionals in acquiring a needed new skill set. Collaboration and distributed leadership is the cornerstone of these efforts and lay a foundation for meaningful change. Grassroots efforts that engaged parents and students, whose advocacy and peer-to-peer networking pushed leadership to effect change.

Key Concepts Discussed

■ Historical context for students who experience intellectual disability gaining access to inclusive higher education.
■ Policies and practices that create access to higher education for students who experience intellectual disability (e.g., grassroots efforts, empowering students with leadership skills, and engaging parents, collaboration and distributive leadership, formation of an interagency taskforce).
■ In-service and pre-service preparation for professionals who support students who experience intellectual disability during their transition from high school to all aspects of adult life including higher education.

Useful Websites

■ Association on Higher Education And Disability https:// www.ahead.org/home
  AHEAD is a United Stares national membership organization that provides resources for disability resource professionals, student affairs personnel, ADA coordinators, diversity officers, AT/IT staff, faculty and other instructional personnel, and colleagues who are invested in creating welcoming higher education experiences for individuals with disability.
■ Minnesota Parent Training and Information Center http:// www.pacer.org
  PACER Center enhances the quality of life and expands opportunities for children, youth, and young adults with all disabilities and their families so each person can reach his or her highest potential. PACER operates on the principles of parents helping parents, supporting families, promoting a safe environment for all children, and working in collaboration with others.

- National Center for College Students with Disabilities
  http://www.nccsdonline.org
  The national center serves college undergraduate and graduate students with *any* type of disability, such as a chronic health condition, or mental or emotional illness. They provide technical assistance at no charge.
- National Technical Assistance Center on Transition https://www.transitionta.org
  NTACT's purpose is to assist State Education Agencies, Local Education Agencies, State VR agencies, and VR service providers in implementing evidence-based and promising practices ensuring students with disabilities, including those with significant disabilities, graduate prepared for success in postsecondary education and employment.
- Think College www.thinkcollege.net
  Think College is a United States national organization dedicated to developing, expanding, and improving inclusive higher education options for people who experience intellectual disability. With a commitment to equity and excellence, Think College supports evidence-based and student-centered research and practice by generating and sharing knowledge, guiding institutional change, informing public policy, and engaging with students, professionals, and families.

Resources

- Grigal, M., Madaus, J., Dukes, L., and Hart, D. (2018). *Navigating the Transition from High School to College for Students with Disabilities*. Milton Park, United Kingdom: Taylor and Francis.
- Jones, M., Boyle, M., May, C., Prohn, S., Updike, J., and Wheeler, C. (2015). Building Inclusive Campus Communities: A Framework for Inclusion. *Think College*

Insight Brief. Issue No. 26. Boston, MA: University of Massachusetts Boston, Institute for Community Inclusion.
▪ Think College National Coordinating Center. (2018). Higher education access for students who experience intellectual disability in the United States. *Think College Snapshot.* May 2018. Boston, MA: University of Massachusetts Boston, Institute for Community Inclusion.

References

Bierly, C., Doyle, B. and Smith, A. (2016). Transforming schools: How distributed leadership can create more high-performing schools. *Bain and Company.* Online: Available at: http://www.bain.com/publications/articles/transforming-schools.aspx. Accessed 15 October 2018.

Boyle, M. (2013). *Universal Design: A Think College Learn Module.* Boston, MA: University of Massachusetts Boston, Institute for Community Inclusion.

Commonwealth of Massachusetts (2012). Senate passes transition services legislation for students with special needs. [Press release]. Online: Available at: http://massadvocates.org/wp-content/uplo ads/Senate-President-Press-Release.pdf. Accessed 15 October 2018.

Council for Exceptional Children (2013). Specialty set: CEC advanced special education transition specialist. *CEC Transition Standards.* Online: Available at: http://community.cec.sped.org/dcdt/cec-transition-standards. Accessed 15 October 2018.

Dwyre, A., Grigal, M. and Fialka, J. (2010). Student and family perspectives. In: M. Grigal and D. Hart (Eds.) *Think College! Postsecondary Options for Students with Intellectual Disabilities.* Baltimore, MD: Paul H. Brookes Publishing Co. pp. 189–227.

Executive Office of Education (2017). Massachusetts inclusive concurrent enrollment. *Massachusetts Department of Higher Education.* Online: Available at: http://www.mass.edu/strategic/read_maicei.asp. Accessed 15 October 2018.

Federation for Children with Special Needs (no date). *Planning a Life* [Publication series]. Boston: FCSN. Online: Available at: https://fcsn.org/linkcenter/. Accessed 15 October 2018.

Freedman, B. (2017). Parent engagement in postsecondary education. Conference presentation at the *D.R.E.A.M. Partnership 3rd*

184 ■ *Leadership for Intellectual Disability Service*

Annual Post-Secondary Education Symposium. Harrisburg, PA. Online: Available at: http://dreampartnership.org/wp-content/uploads/2013/04/PA-PSE-Symposium-2017-Family-Engagement-Brian-Freedman.pdf. Accessed 15 October 2018.

Gordon, K. (2015). Bedford resident testifies on Beacon Hill. *The Bedford Citizen.* Online: Available at: https://www.thebedfo rdcitizen.org/2015/10/bedford-resident-testifies-on-beacon-hill. Accessed 15 October 2018.

Harris, A. (2014). Distributed leadership. *Teacher Magazine.* Online: Available at: https://www.teachermagazine.com.au/articles/distri buted-leadership. Accessed 15 October 2018.

Hart, D., Simeone, M., Wilczenski, F. and Paiewonsky, M. (2013). School district/college partnerships for inclusive dual enrollment college options. Conference presentation. *Inclusive Higher Education Conference.* Washington, DC.

Hart, D., Zafft, C. and Zimbrich, K. (2001). Creating access to college for all students. *Journal for Vocational Special Needs 23*(2), 19–31.

Hooley, R. and Cardoza, H. (2018). Robert's passion for theatre put him on the path to college. *Think College Transition Student Profiles.* Issue No. 2. Boston, MA: University of Massachusetts Boston, Institute for Community Inclusion.

Landau, J. (2011). Youth with disabilities, parents, educators, join legislators to urge support for legislation to promote jobs and independence for youth with disabilities. [Press release.] Boston, MA: Massachusetts Advocates for Children.

Love, M.L., Baker, J.N. and Devine, S. (2017). Universal design for learning: Supporting college inclusion for students with intellectual disabilities. *Career Development and Transition for Exceptional Individuals.* doi: https://doi.org/10.1177/2165143417722518

Martinez, D., Conroy, J. and Cerreto, M. (2012). Parent involvement in the transition process of children with intellectual disabilities: The influence of inclusion on parent desires and expectations for postsecondary education. *Journal of Policy and Practice in Intellectual Disabilities 9*(4), 279–288.

Massachusetts Advocates for Children (no date). *Transition.* Online: Available at: https://massadvocates.org/transition. Accessed 15 October 2018.

Massachusetts Advocates for Children (2018). *Young adult leaders fellowship: Maximo Pimentel.* Online: Available at: https://ma ssadvocates.org/young-adult-leaders-fellowship-maximo-piment el. Accessed 15 October 2018.

Massachusetts Department of Elementary and Secondary Education (no date). *School and district profiles.* [Data file]. Online: Available at: http://profiles.doe.mass.edu. Accessed 15 October 2018.

Massachusetts Department of Elementary and Secondary Education (2015). *Regulations for educator licensure and preparation program approval, 603 CMR 7.14, transition specialist endorsement.* Online: Available at: http://bit.ly/1JUxfvb. Accessed 15 October 2018.

Massachusetts Department of Elementary and Secondary Education (2016). *Report to the legislature: Inclusive concurrent enrollment partnership programs for students with disabilities.* Malden, MA: Massachusetts Department of Elementary and Secondary Education.

Massachusetts House and Senate Co-Chairs of the Joint Committee on Higher Education (2014). *A taskforce on higher education for students with intellectual disability and autism spectrum disorder: A report to the Massachusetts legislature.* Online: Available at: https://massadvocates.org/wp-content/uploads/Higher-Ed-Final-task-force-report-4-14-2.pdf. Accessed 15 October 2018.

Massachusetts Legislature (2011). *An act to promote the successful transition of students with disabilities to post-secondary education, employment, and independent living* (H.3720). Fact sheet. Online: Available at: http://massadvocates.org/wp-content/uploads/Factsheet.pdf. Accessed 15 October 2018.

National Technical Assistance Center on Transition (2016). *Effective Practices and Predictors Matrix.* Charlotte, NC: NTACT.

Norton, M. (2014). *Task Force Urges Inclusion of Students with Disabilities in Higher Education.* Boston, MA: State House News Service.

Paiewonsky, M., Boyle, M., Hanson, T., Price, P., MacDonald, P. and Schwartz, S. (2013). Establishing inclusive postsecondary education opportunities: Tips for effective communication. *Think College Insight Brief.* Issue No. 20. Boston, MA: University of Massachusetts Boston, Institute for Community Inclusion.

Paiewonsky, M., Hanson, T., Dashzeveg, O. and Western Massachusetts Student Researchers (2017). Put yourself on the map: Inclusive research with and by college students with intellectual disability/autism. *Student Reports: A Think College Transition Brief.* Boston, MA: University of Massachusetts Boston, Institute for Community Inclusion.

Paiewonsky, M. and Roach Ostergard, J. (2010). Local school system perspectives. In: M. Grigal and D. Hart (Eds.) *Think College! Postsecondary Education Options for Students with Intellectual Disabilities.* Baltimore, MD: Paul H. Brookes Publishing Co. pp. 87–160.

Paiewonsky, M., Sroka, A. Ahearn, M., Santucci, A., Quiah, G., Bauer, C., … Lee, W. (2010). Think, hear, see, believe college: Students using participatory action research to document the college experience. *Think College Insight Brief.* Issue No. 5. Boston, MA: Institute for Community Inclusion, University of Massachusetts Boston.

Plotner, A.J. and Simonsen, M.L. (2018). Examining federally funded secondary transition personnel preparation programs. *Career Development and Transition for Exceptional Individuals 41*(1), 39–49.

Quinn, C. (2013). *College Grant Program Touted for Benefits to Disabled Students.* Boston, MA: State House News Service.

Rossetti, Z., Lehr, D., Pelerin, D., Shuoxi, H., Lederer, L. and Huang, S. (2016). Parent involvement in meaningful post-school experiences for young adults with IDD and pervasive support needs. *Intellectual and Developmental Disabilities 54*(4), 260–272.

Think College: Program Database (2003). Online database. Online: Available at: http://thinkcollege.net. Accessed 15 October 2018.

University of Massachusetts Boston (2018). Graduate certificate in special education with a concentration in transition leadership. Online: Available at: https://www.umb.edu/academics/cehd/curriculum/grad/special_education_med/transition_leadership Accessed 15 October 2018.

Weber, A. (2015). The young adult leaders fellowship: Effecting change in Massachusetts. *Institute Brief.* Issue No. 33. Boston, MA: University of Massachusetts Boston, Institute for Community Inclusion.

Weir, C. (2013). *For Families: Options and Planning for College. A Think College Learn Module.* Boston, MA: University of Massachusetts Boston, Institute for Community Inclusion.

Wetherby, S. and Hanson, T. (2015). Becoming an anime artist: My experience at college. *Think College Stories.* Boston, MA: University of Massachusetts Boston, Institute for Community Inclusion.

Yarborough, D., Getzel, E., and Kester, J. (2014). *Expectations of families with young adults with intellectual and developmental disabilities for postsecondary education.* Topical paper. Richmond, VA: Center for Transition Innovations, Virginia Commonwealth University.

APPLICATION

Chapter 8

Leadership in Practice: Four Participatory Vignettes

Colin Griffiths

Contents

Chapter Topics

- Examines four exemplars of how leadership can be enacted in the everyday interactions between practitioners and those in receipt of their service.
- Considers areas such as nursing, education and the management of change at a macro level.
- Encourages readers to reflect on the value of participation in contemporary leadership.

Introduction

This chapter seeks to provide illustrative evidence of how leadership that is not wholly driven from the top may emerge and may operate to promote the good for those who are supported by services. In order to do this, four exemplars are offered, each in their own way telling a story of how people who are *doing the job* seek to do what they and others do in a better way and in a manner that makes their interventions more effective, with the ultimate aim of improving the life quality of those whom they are serving. All exemplars are concerned with developing new and innovative approaches to dealing with existing problems so, in many ways; they can be seen as people thinking things through differently in order to bring about change. Of great importance is that the chosen mechanisms are developed by the people upon whom the responsibility for re-engineering the system lies. Furthermore, those people are not necessarily in positions of great power, they are simply people in various levels within an organisation who are doing the best they can and, in doing so, engaging in leadership.

The exemplars were drawn from different support modes: nursing; education; and management. Each explores the context within which the changes took place, the nature of the changes and draws out the key lessons learned.

Exemplar 1: Nurse Managers Get It Together

Lorraine Ledger, Anne-Marie O'Reilly

The first exemplar is taken from a high-support service based in Ireland and looks at how the requirement for a nursing structure arose in that service. It demonstrates how service users' health needs contributed to the implementation of person-focussed initiatives. A straightforward example of how things should be done, some might say; however, as those who have worked in large services will attest, getting meaningful change underway is not always easy. This example gives some idea of how, and in what context, such change may be achieved.

An organisation is an entity with a collective goal. Organisations providing residential and respite care for people with an intellectual disability should be focused on ensuring that individual needs are met on a twenty-four-hour basis. Often, however, service provision, multidisciplinary teams, management and governing structures are provided during office hours only, on a Monday to Friday basis, with little support for the remaining hours of the week. A large community-based organisation in Ireland utilised the skills of Registered Intellectual Disability Nurses (RNID) to develop and lead innovation in the provision of intellectual disability service.

This organisation, established in 1955, was the initiative of likeminded parents who wanted an alternative type of care for their family members to that provided by large institutions, which were the models of service at that time. It initially offered day services, but over the years and due to the changing demands of service users, it has expanded to provide a large range of services to more than 1,700 people; this includes residential and respite care, across 78 houses in the greater Dublin region. The skill mix of front line staff is premised on the needs of the service users, with social care being the dominant professional group. However, due to the changing ageing profile and complex needs of both older and younger service users, there was a recognition that more RNIDs were required.

As far back as 2002, an audit of out-of-hours queries, triaged by managers from varying skill mixes and professional backgrounds, demonstrated that many such managers felt unable to deal with some of the queries, as they did not have a nursing background.

In 2003, the nurse manager on call (NMOC) service was initiated to address all nursing and managerial issues. The NMOC team provides a 24-hour, 365-day-a-year, seamless service with a telephone triage and clinical frontline engagement from 17.00 hrs to 09.00 hrs. The team comprises four nurses, all of whom are RNIDs. There is an NMOC available at all times, and the role is administratively positioned between managerial and front line teams. This exclusive position within the organisational structure has allowed the NMOC team to become autonomous practitioners. It offers the broader team an insight into the organisational challenges and complexities involved in addressing service users' unique needs. Through nursing leadership, the NMOC has influenced service provision to promote a more person-centred service.

Accessing generic services can be difficult for people with an intellectual disability, as information and guidance may not be available in accessible formats. Furthermore, early ageing within this population may preclude them from taking part in appropriate national health promotion programmes. The NMOC have led out on a number of relevant initiatives. For example, they developed nurse-led phlebotomy clinics with accessible information for service users. These have been very successful, as they have provided clinical services in familiar environments, which have resulted in reduced anxiety for many. There are seven such clinics running monthly, in three different regions across the organisation. They also offer the opportunity for the NMOCs to supervise and mentor nurses, newly trained in phlebotomy.

Through enhanced knowledge, skills and formal education, the NMOC has devised individualised care plans and educational packages for service users, their families and front line staff. These packages cover topics such as diabetes, constipation, pain and bone health. They are developed with service users, based on best practice and contemporary research evidence.

A bone health and falls awareness initiative was developed to support people with an intellectual disability to maintain the best bone health possible throughout their lifespan. The initiative, Happy Bones (www.happybones.ie), is a good example of nurses leading change within intellectual disability. It has generated a lot of interest both nationally and internationally. This resource has resulted in an increased awareness of the importance of good bone health, falls awareness and falls prevention strategies among all age groups and has generated an increase in the numbers of people with an intellectual disability being referred for osteoporosis screening and receiving recommended interventions. Intellectual disability nurses are well placed to influence service provision, national policy and to coordinate care in partnership with people with an intellectual disability.

In these initiatives, nurses recognised a need for practice change and subsequently approached senior managers in the service with a detailed analysis of the problems that had to be addressed. Benefits included enhanced care and support, changes in practice and cost efficiency. Such grass roots approaches where staff participate in the change process are indicative of a commitment to a distributed approach to leadership.

Exemplar 2: Reflective Teamwork, Supporting Classroom Leadership for Inclusion

Anna Logan

The next exemplar is from the education sector and is concerned with how decision-making regarding the needs of one pupil may, through teamwork, be adapted for the benefit of other students. This collaborative approach is illustrated and a framework of reflective teamwork is identified as a useful tool through which mutual trust is engendered between the participants. The initiative was instigated by the class teacher *Catherine* when she began working for the first time with *Linda*, a special needs assistant (SNA) appointed to provide support for *Edel*, a seven-year-old pupil with a mild general intellectual disability and severe hearing loss. Pseudonyms are used to protect the identity of those involved.

At an initial meeting prior to the beginning of the new school year, Catherine invited Linda to engage with her weekly in 15-minute sessions using a reflective teamwork model for teacher/ assistant partnership (Cremin et al., 2005). Reflective teamwork, which involves brief training in teamwork skills, including establishing ground rules, the use of non-judgemental language, active listening, questioning, giving feedback and problem-solving, has been positively evaluated by both teachers and SNAs in a small study in two Irish primary schools (O'Brien, 2010).

Catherine had been introduced to this model and the underpinning teamwork skills while completing postgraduate studies in inclusive and special education during the previous academic year. When she suggested using this approach to discussing and planning how they might work together as a team, Linda was open to the idea. They agreed to meet for 15 minutes each Thursday, immediately after school. The first six minutes involved each partner identifying two things that went well and two that did not go well during the previous week. After this, they each summarised what the other had said. In the remaining nine minutes, they brainstormed, evaluated and agreed targets and planned work for the coming week.

Referring to her previous experience working with an SNA, Catherine noted that:

> *People have different working styles; it can just take a while and there is a period of adjustment every year, maybe a month or two at the beginning of the year.*

It's sometimes a bit awkward with someone new in
your room ... you're used to doing things in one way
and they're used to doing things a different way, a
particular way.

Furthermore, Catherine had no previous experience of
teaching pupils with significant hearing loss but was aware
that Linda had supported Edel during the previous school
year and had completed two introductory Irish Sign Language
courses with her. Therefore, she was motivated to use the
reflective teamwork model to establish a framework whereby
they could share expertise, jointly plan and decide how to best
support Edel's inclusion in the classroom. Catherine noted:

To be honest I was really worried about how I would
communicate with Edel. I don't know any signs and I
knew that there was going to be a sound field system
in the classroom which stressed me out a bit ... Linda
has lots of experience, I know she has sign language
and she worked with Edel last year so I really wanted
to learn from her. I suppose I hoped we'd figure out
together how best to meet Edel's needs and then I
thought about the reflective teamwork idea.

Having used the reflective teamwork model weekly during
the first school term, she further commented:

I feel like we're working together as a team. Linda is
very proactive, making suggestions, commenting and
we can discuss something together and come up with
a solution together ... she would know the child best
as well ... you know she spends more time with Edel
than I do so I would really take on board anything
she says ... If you are working as a team you need to
be able to rely on someone ... I really appreciate her
coming back to me and letting me know the things

that are working and the things that they are finding difficult.

Likewise, identifying that *'there's always a settling in period when you're starting to work with a different teacher'* Linda outlined how the reflective teamwork supported shared reflection and evaluation:

We go through what works; what doesn't work. We identify any problems, any issues, we go back to the drawing board, see if we could have done something different. Like yesterday I was saying that with the video it was maybe a bit long.

Both Linda and Catherine identified the benefits for pupils and for themselves.

We set clear goals and we achieve them, we are on the same page and we have high expectations for the pupils. We get to share plans, get a lot of information and feedback from each other as well. It's all about feedback!

(Linda)

Pupils make more progress when everyone is working together ... it makes for a nicer school experience and learning environment for the child and there is good continuity and flow. We get support when things are difficult, and it's great just bouncing ideas off her and learning from the other person.

(Catherine)

The impact of mutual understanding and shared high expectations was evident in the classroom. For example, both Catherine and Linda were concerned that Edel would become

increasingly independent in the care and management of her
hearing aid and processor, as Linda noted:

Initially I used to do all that for her, now we are
trying to wean her off that support so that she can
become independent.

Establishing shared expectations is a key factor in achieving
greater autonomy and empowerment for those working with
children and adolescents who have disabilities.

Policy relating to SNAs (Department of Education and
Skills, 2014) may be argued to be principally focused on
functions, behaviours and tasks. An overriding concern has
been to delineate the care role of the SNA from the teaching and learning remit of the teachers with whom they work
(Logan, 2008). This is perhaps reflective of the hierarchical and
bureaucratic nature of schools, the relatively low status of the
SNA and a focus on maintaining the *status quo* (Gumus et al.,
2018). In contrast, this exemplar illustrates the positive outcomes of leadership that can originate in an individual classroom, motivated by teacher interest in inclusive practice and
exemplifying shared learning and leadership by both teacher
and SNA. This, in turn, paves the way for the development of
inclusive classroom practice.

Understandably, teachers are often focused on practice
within their own classroom rather than change and improvement at a school or system level (Kitching et al., 2009). In initiating reflective teamwork with Linda, Catherine demonstrated
leadership, creating conditions conducive to mutual learning,
problem-solving and decision-making. However, the exemplar also illustrates that this was not a top-down, hierarchical
approach since both Linda and Catherine brought different
and complementary knowledge and skills to the partnership.
As such, it can be considered participative, in that leadership was shared and exercised collectively rather than vested
in a single authority (Gumus et al., 2018). A recent review of

research relating to leadership models in education highlighted an increased focus on leadership involving people from all grades and levels.

At the end of the 2017/18 school year, 14,100 SNAs were employed in Irish schools. Working in very close relationships with pupils and teachers, they play a key role in supporting inclusion in education and empowerment of children and young people with special educational needs. This exemplar has demonstrated the potential of models such as reflective teamwork to enhance leadership and collaboration within classroom teams and challenge existing policy and practice at both school and system level.

Exemplar 3: Developing Young Adult Leadership among Self-Advocates

Maximo Pimentel

The third exemplar, also in the field of education, explores the role of student advocates in assisting other older students with intellectual disability to take control of their lives.

In Massachusetts, United States, advocates work to promote the rights of young people with intellectual and developmental disability to access inclusive postsecondary education. Their success has been attributed to a grassroots collaboration between legislative and legal advocates, researchers, families and young adults with disabilities themselves. In fact, the influence that young college student advocates have had on state legislators, who have been impressed with their stories, led one special education advocacy organisation, Mass. Advocates for Children, to develop a Young Adult Leaders Fellowship. Through these one-year fellowships, one young adult fellow every year is included in all aspects of educational advocacy: meeting with state legislators; working with families and students to ensure that educational plans are leading to inclusive outcomes; and providing training to stakeholders including families, teachers and younger students who are preparing for their transition from school to young adult life.

One Young Adult Leader Fellow, Maximo Pimentel (24), is committed to helping younger students with disabilities to take steps, in as early as high school, to advocate for their dreams through educational planning meetings (IEP or Individual Education Programme meetings). For the last two years, Maximo has been meeting with students in Boston Public High Schools, encouraging them to speak up, know their rights and persevere to reach their goals. What follows is an interview conducted with Maximo about his advocacy experience.

When asked to explain the advocacy work that he has been doing, Maximo responded: *I started advocacy work three years ago. I started it because I was in a program for students with disabilities, getting support to go to college. When the program was done, the director of the program invited me to a college night and asked me to share my experience. I was a veteran at that. But I didn't know how to do presentations and I had never talked in public before. I said 'Why not' and I did it. Since then I have done advocacy for the Massachusetts Inclusive Concurrent Enrolment Initiative (MAICEI). I also keep talking to high school students about speaking up at their own IEP meetings and about my own experiences in the Boston Public Schools and college. I am working to motivate them to advocate for themselves and get support to go to college as well.*

Maximo was asked about his work for Mass Advocates for Children: *I was a Young Adult Fellow at Mass Advocates for Children (MAC) for a year. There I learned how laws are made and also, I learned how to speak up for myself and also for others. I went with the MAC staff to the Massachusetts State House and learned how to advocate with state senators and house representatives about bills and asking to sponsor bills. I also did a lot of office work and I did a lot of training with staff to explain to parents how they can be more involved with their child with special needs.*

When I started at Bunker Hill (local community college involved in MAICEI), I started as a business major but after I started at Mass Advocates for Children and saw all their amazing work, I decided to switch my major from business to human services. I realized that people helping me when I was in high school was what I wanted to now do for others in high school.

Explaining what it was like to talk to state legislatures about his experiences, he replied: *It's very interesting because they get to see from a different point of view what it's like and also, they are impressed with the students who talk to them with their stories. They feel connected. Also, they are more willing to listen. Many times, students with disabilities have successful stories and those are the ones they want to hear.*

Recalling that many advocates feel that inclusive college opportunities opened in Massachusetts because there were all kinds of people coming together to advocate for changes, it was noted that legislative advocates, research advocates and education advocates are needed. Maximo was asked if he could have been this successful if we didn't have student advocates. He explained: *Well, the advocates who were not students were doing a great job but the impact that student advocates bring to the table is huge. It's because students know how it feels to have so much on their plate. Also, it makes a huge impression, an impact, if the students are advocating for themselves along with their fellow advocates. It just makes it a big deal.*

Maximo considered what could be done to prepare more young people to advocate like him: *First of all, I think we need more youth to train trainers how to tell the story and show young advocates how to tell their story in their own unique way, different from other advocates. We also need more involvement from students with disabilities. There are still just a few students with disabilities involved and I feel like we need*

*more youth trainers willing to speak up for themselves and
share their stories.*

He reflected on what he would do with his new skills:
*What I would like to do with my advocacy and leadership skills
is to show students with disabilities that whatever they have in
mind, whatever their goal is, it's possible. I want to continue
concentrating on students in their schools, to help them transition from high school to college or whatever they want to do
after school. With my leadership skills and my advocacy skills, I
want them to be successful, just like I am.*

Finally, he explained what key knowledge was required by
students with intellectual disability: *I think the most important
thing that a person with a disability needs to know and understand is that their opinion matters and that their rights matter
as well. Just because they are a person with a disability doesn't
mean that they can't contribute to society. They just need to
find their passion and their courage to change the world.*

Maximo offers a powerful example of how people themselves can change things. He reminds us that, in the final
analysis, the person with an intellectual disability is the
expert on *their* intellectual disability and it is from them that
change must come. However, for many, especially those with
more severe intellectual disability staff (along with families)
are proxy advocates. How then can staff be enabled to lead
change and develop quality services?

Exemplar 4: Every Which Way Including Loose

Brendan Broderick

The final exemplar taken from the managerial sector
attempts to answer that question. In this exemplar the Chief
Executive Officer of a service for people with an intellectual
disability recounts how he tried and failed to bring about
top-down change in policy and practice in a large organisation. The main lessons seem to be that, once staff have been

launched on a trajectory for change, a balance has to be found between trusting them to get it (nearly) right and enabling them to create their own solutions while, at the same time, engineering a loose system of guidelines.

The large Irish service of which I am CEO made a number of false starts between 2007 and 2009 at installing an element of tailored individualised support within our general array of services. The aspiration was to embed within the various adult day and residential centres a range of individualised support arrangements; a number of satellite support arrangements which were radically personalised, forming part of the mix alongside a fairly conventional constellation of group-based arrangements. The presumption was that a number of care-fully selected *innovation champions* would be able to launch and sustain these initiatives alongside and parallel to their routine responsibilities. It was a classic top-down approach. I had been an ardent promoter of 'one person at a time' arrangements and had been intermittently seeking to ani-mate initiatives that would seed this orientation within the general landscape. Typically, these initiatives would take off with enthusiasm and commitment. However, after three to four months, they would generally lose altitude on the prior-ity radar as well as traction on the ground, leaving a legacy of pessimism and hopelessness.

Jumping ahead. Eight years later, we now have about 50 radically individualised person-centred arrangements in place, almost half of which involve 24/7 supports. A significant num-ber involve 30–50 hours of support during the week. The peo-ple supported include many with very significant and complex needs. The arrangements are exclusively bespoke and individ-ualised; no one is ever supported, even briefly or incidentally, in group contexts. The focus is on the individual's aspirations and priorities in the context of 'the life you want for yourself', rather than on the more paternalistic construct of 'your needs' (the shift from 'servicing needs' to 'getting a life' is critical). The practice model which has evolved has significant mileage on the clock and has progressed well beyond the pilot stage. The majority of arrangements have been in place for more than five years and the teams have displayed impressive resilience and adaptive agility in absorbing and responding to various challenges and crises. Many of the approximately 100 staff members involved in direct support had no disability sector background (either via training or experience). Moreover, the aggregate cost of supporting individuals in this way compares very favourably with costs associated with conventional group-based models.

What happened to launch and sustain this initiative? A pivotal turning point was the recognition by two regional directors that (a) the attempt to force change centrally, and from the top, lacked the organisational horsepower to deliver this kind of embedded long-haul change and (b) seeking to run this initiative alongside conventional commitments would inevitably result in it losing out to immediate, often reactive, events. They proposed that the innovation needed 'clear blue water' between it and the mothership organisation – and should be the exclusive responsibility of one of the regional directors. Accordingly, we set about recruiting a team of internal 'vision champions' to drive the initiative. Insight into vision and passionate commitment to make a difference were the main attributes sought in the vision champions. The belief that 'if you don't *get it*, you can't pass it on' was central. The recruitment phase was followed by an extended formation phase (much broader and deeper than a skills-acquisition training focus) consisting of extended inputs from two external consultants over two to three months focusing on: fidelity to vision; authentic modes of communication and engagement; self-awareness; negotiating common ground with the individual and his/her family; and navigating within a context of uncertainty and emergent design. Following this period of formation, coordinators were linked with individuals. The leadership orientation was focused on how best to nurture, support, develop and facilitate this key group. Formal goal setting, as in the identification of milestone targets, key performance indicators and other performance-management measures, was consciously avoided. It was recognised that the process of working with these individuals was inherently open-ended, creative and emergent. Supporting coordinators to keep faith with vision during intervals when it was not at all clear what specific direction to take, the equivalent of 'blank page anxiety', to continue probing for the most productive channels and not to 'earth' tension and anxiety by opting for the safe harbour of plausible activity was paramount. Sustaining courage, fortitude and creativity would determine whether we would be successful. This required supportive confidence-building mentoring where cultivating an ethic of optimism was essential. Baroness Shirley Williams' (2018) observation that leadership is about participation, not command resonates.

No explicit theory of leadership underpinned or guided the delivery of this initiative. There were some related beliefs and precepts that informed how we went about it and an implicit leadership orientation and temperament is probably identifiable. Core to our thinking was a recognition that grounded vision, imagination and creative problem solving does not lodge neatly within the upper echelons of conventional hierarchies; we needed to create an approach to engaging with staff at all levels that incentivised them to exercise their own discretion, supported local experimentation and allowed us to catalyse and capture the creativity distributed across the organisation. The avoidance of top-down grand plans and associated command-and-control orientations was central to ensuring that local actors had the discretionary space to improvise self-authored solutions.

Subsequently, we have come across various writers in whose work we recognise strong affinities with the way we have approached this initiative. Foremost among these has been the *experimentalist governance* approach developed by Sabel and Zeitlin (2012). The role taken on by central leadership within this paradigm is one of identifying broad framework goals linked to provisional goal setting. Local units have the discretion to pursue these goals in their own way but, as a condition of the autonomy granted to them, are expected to report on their performance, participate in peer view and incorporate the learning evidenced in other better performing local actors. This approach values provoking doubt about one's own assumptions and urges that all *solutions* be approached as incomplete and capable of being enhanced. It recognises that fixed rules written by a hierarchical authority are prone to become obsolete and superseded by changing dynamics and local context. The critical justification of local action is 'whether it advances organisational purpose and not whether it is rule compliant'. Some parallels with Donald Rumsfeld's reiteration of von Moltke's famous statement that 'no plan survives contact with the enemy'! The work of John Seddon and the *Vanguard* method (Vanguard, 2016) urging an unwavering focus on core purpose was also very helpful in ensuring that we did not succumb to the distractions of task fragmentation, fixation with process or getting duped into responding to *failure demand*, while remaining open to the learning of those at the coalface. Otto Scharmer's (2018) referencing of the four levels of listening (downloading, factual listening, empathic listening and generative listening) and William Isaacs' (1999) promotion of conversational and dialogical approaches also provoked flashes of recognition.

Conclusion

Although the four exemplars are taken from very different situations where people with an intellectual disability are supported, the overall theme that links them is that working out solutions for (and with) people with an intellectual disability is best done by those who are directly engaged with the person or by those who are aligned to the persons themselves. This means that leadership rests with the people who are actually doing the work. It also suggests that teamwork is of critical importance. What motivates these staff to try to think through new solutions to old problems? The reader can delve into these exemplars to discover their own answers but some might think that trust, teamwork, collaboration and a valuing of the person, to the extent that one feels that he or she deserves better, are component parts of the whole.

Finally, some lessons can be drawn from these exemplars. Staff must have the capacity to analyse, consider and reflect upon the needs of people and current practices that operate to serve them. Furthermore, the proximity of staff and others to the problem or matter in question is of great importance, because those in direct contact with individuals who require new solutions are the people with the knowledge of what works and what does not and hence, are more likely to be able to devise solutions to those problems. This is what leadership is all about: namely, bottom-up solutions and initiatives that challenge the *status quo* through intimate knowledge of the problem or issue that is to be addressed.

Key Concepts Discussed

- Participative leadership.
- Special needs education.
- Person-centred support.
- Reflection.

Useful Websites/Key Readings

- Exemplar 1.
    For more information on Happy Bones see www. happybones.ie
- Exemplar 2.
    For more information on inclusive education see: Department of Education and Skills (2014) *The Special*

Needs Assistant (SNA) scheme to support teachers in meeting the care needs of some children with special educational needs, arising from a disability. Online: Available at: https://www.sess.ie/sites/default/files/DES%20Circular_0030_2014.pdf Accessed 19 October 2018.

■ Exemplar 3.

For more information about the Mass Advocates for Children Young Adult Leaders Fellowship, check out this brief: Weber, A. (2015). The Young Adult Leaders Fellowship: Effecting Change in Massachusetts. *The Institute Brief.* University of MA Boston, Issue 33 Online: Available at: https://massadvocates.org/wp-content/uploads/IB33_F3.pdf. Accessed 19 October 2018.

■ Exemplar 4.

For more information on managerial approaches to distributed leadership see: The Design Gym. Online: Available at: http://www.thedesigngym.com/the-four-levels-of-listening-how-you-can-listen-your-way-to-innovation/Accessed 19 October 2018.

Experimentalist Governance. Online: Available at: https://www.researchgate.net/profile/Charles_Sabel/publication/228435683_Experimentalist_Governance/links/00463520ea077a6846000000.pdf. Accessed 19 October 2018.

References

Cremin, H., Thomas, G. and Vincett, K. (2005). Working with teaching assistants: Three models evaluated. *Research Papers in Education 20*(4), 413–432.

Gumus, S., Bellibas, M.S., Esen, M. and Gumus, E. (2018). A systematic review of studies on leadership models in educational research from 1980 to 2014. *Educational Management Administration and Leadership 46*(1), 25–48.

Isaacs, W. (1999). *Dialogue and the Art of Thinking Together.* New York, NY: Bantam Doubleday Dell Publishing Group.

Kitching, K., O' Leary, M. and Morgan, M. (2009). It's the little things: Exploring the importance of commonplace events for early-career teachers' motivation. *Teachers and Teaching 15*(1), 43–58.

Logan, A. (2008). Special needs and children's right to be heard under the UN Convention on the Rights of the Child 1989 in the Republic of Ireland. *Education Law Journal 9*(2), 107–118.

O'Brien, E. (2010). Teachers and special needs assistants in Irish classrooms: An evaluation of a model of reflective teamwork. *Reach Journal of Special Needs Education in Ireland 23*(2), 81–94.

Sabel, C.F. and Zeitlin, J. (2012). Experimentalist governance In: D. Levi-Faur (Ed.) *The Oxford Handbook of Governance*. Oxford: Oxford University Press. pp. 169–186.

Scharmer, O. (2018). *The Essentials of Theory. U.* Oalkand, CA: Berrett-Koehler Publishers.

Seddon, J. (2016). What Is the Vanguard Method? *Vanguard*. Online: Available at: https://vanguard-method.net/welcome-and-what-is-the-vanguard-method-best-2. Accessed 15 October 2018.

Williams, S. (2018). Shirley Williams Conversations. Online: Available at: https://subsaga.com/bbc/politics/conversations/shirley-williams.html. Accessed 15 October 2018.

Index

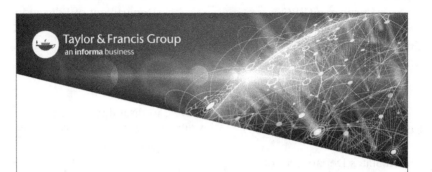